AUTHOR	CLASS
MARSHALL, J. D.	E
TITLE Lancashire	No.
	4908874 6

D0475874

LANCASHIRE

CITY AND COUNTY HISTORIES

General Editor: Lionel Munby
Board of Extra-Mural Studies,
University of Cambridge
Editor of *The Local Historian*

Published

DORSET	J. H. Bettey
TYNESIDE	C. M. Fraser and K. Emsley

In preparation

CORNWALL	Lawrence S. Snell
DERBYSHIRE	John Heath
DURHAM	B. K. Roberts
GLAMORGAN	John Davies
NOTTINGHAM	Alan Rogers
THE POTTERIES	Michael Greenslade and Denis Stuart
SOMERSET	R. W. Dunning
SOUTH YORKSHIRE	Derek Holland
SUFFOLK	John Ridgard
SURREY	A. R. and R. A. Michell
TEESSIDE	Barry Harrison

CITY AND COUNTY HISTORIES

LANCASHIRE

J. D. MARSHALL

DAVID & CHARLES
Newton Abbot   London
North Pomfret (VT)   Vancouver

ISBN 0 7153 6653 X

0190135 2
49088746

Set in 12pt on 13pt Aldine Bembo
and printed in Great Britain
by Latimer Trend & Company Ltd Plymouth
for David & Charles (Holdings) Limited
South Devon House Newton Abbot Devon

Published in the United States of America
by David & Charles Inc
North Pomfret Vermont 05053 USA

Published in Canada
by Douglas David & Charles Limited
3645 McKechnie Drive West Vancouver BC

CONTENTS

LIST OF ILLUSTRATIONS

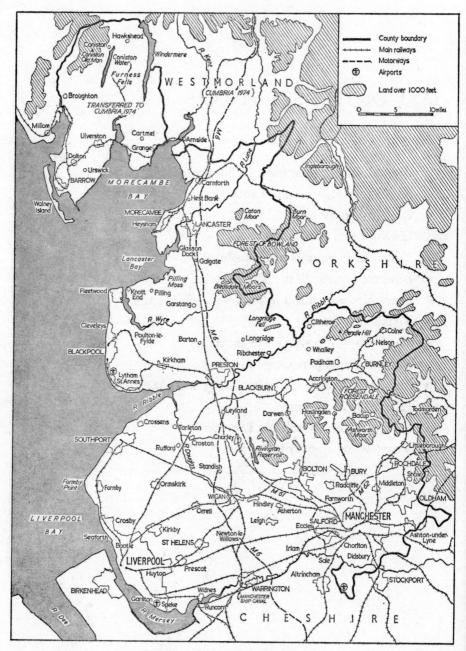

General map of Lancashire

Chapter 1

THE LANCASHIRE OF
THE ARCHAEOLOGIST
AND THE ANTIQUARY

THE HISTORY OF HISTORIANS

THE history of a place, region or county is in reality the creation of its historians. We rely upon them for the innumerable versions of 'what actually happened'. Every county has its historians, and we must learn to look at them critically, just as the reader must regard critically the various statements that are made in this book.

Most of our English counties acquired their historians, or more properly their antiquaries, between the mid-sixteenth and the late eighteenth century. But many more county surveys must have remained unpublished. The physician and scholar, Dr Richard Kuerden of Preston (1623–90?), was encouraged by the great Sir Thomas Dugdale, the historian of Warwickshire, to produce a similar history of Lancashire. But Kuerden was so intimidated by Dugdale's own example that the project came to nothing. The resultant incomplete manuscript came to rest in Chetham's Library, Manchester, and is of very great interest, for it embodies a detailed prospectus of the proposed work (1688). It was to have been a thorough topographical survey of boundaries, roads, rivers and other natural features with (much more important to the mind of the seventeenth-century antiquary) an account of the noble and leading families of the county. Accordingly, Kuerden was to have provided us with 'A Catalogue of such Syrnames as came over with W[illiam] C[onqueror]'.

The very limited subscribing public for such a work was, of

course, to be found among gentle families who looked for a demonstration of the antiquity and respectability of other leading families in the county. The study of local history, or of any kind of history, was still in its infancy, and archaeology was in what we might call its prehistory. Nevertheless, the urge to record the past was a powerful one, and in 1787 a landed gentleman and magistrate of Farnworth near Bolton, named Dorning Rasbotham, collected several volumes of notes with such an end in view. Unfortunately 'his health failed him before his Herculean task was accomplished'.

His notes, however, passed into the hands of Edward Baines, whose massive four-volume *History of the County Palatine and Duchy of Lancaster*, published in 1836, is a monument to nineteenth-century achievement. Lancashire had to wait a long time for this, its first major county history (if we ignore Dr Charles Leigh's *Natural History* of the region, published in 1697), although Thomas West's *Antiquities of Furness* (1774) was a distinguished work which went beyond its nominal aim, that of studying Furness Abbey and the local gentry. Even earlier, too, Lancashire's cultural history was enriched unbeknown by the compilation of John Lucas's *History of Warton* (originated in 1710-40 and published in 1931), one of the most remarkable parish studies of its type to be found anywhere. Liverpool and Manchester acquired their local historians in Enfield (1774) and Whittaker (1771-5) respectively, followed by a succession of local chroniclers in these towns, and by Dr T. D. Whittaker's *History of Whalley and Clitheroe* (1806). Perhaps it is typical of Lancashire that local pride and involvement should come before awareness on a county scale.

Yet Baines's great work was well worth waiting for, and was different from previous county antiquarian studies in one important respect. It was concerned not only with the distant past, or with the landed gentry, or with monuments of different kinds, but with the industrial world which was evolving on all sides. It drew on the comparatively recent development of archaeology, then a very new-fangled study in any systematic sense, and combined this study with an extensive use of local documents and even national archives, so that it included (for example) a literal transcription of the relevant parts of Domesday Book. There were occasional serious attempts to interpret pre-Domesday history. Otherwise Baines's volumes were concerned with descriptive matter, and with institutions, genealogies and biographies.

Very little separates the Baines work, in terms of method and spirit, from the eight-volume *Victoria County History of Lancashire* (1906–14) edited by William Farrer and John Brownbill. Indeed, Baines was in many ways far more aware of the importance of the industrial world of the north, and the earth-shaking events of the nineteenth century were of little significance to these later editors. The *Victoria County History*, following an established pattern, devoted elaborate and systematic scholarship to Lancashire manors, parishes, churches and castles, but provided only the most perfunctory of information about its great towns and their growth. The industrial world appears in the pages of Baines as a positive force.

LAYING BARE THE PAST

It was highly appropriate that Edward Baines should react in this way. The Industrial Revolution, as a changer, a destroyer and an excavator, stimulated interest in the past as it laid the latter bare. The digging of warehouse and other foundations, and the making of roads, canals and railways, led to more and more archaeological 'finds', as the following example shows. The discovery of an apparently Roman water-storage system in Castlefield, Manchester, about 1830, was described in these terms: 'In cutting and carrying away part of Castlefield, to make the ground level near a new warehouse, lately erected on the banks of the canal, a very ancient well was discovered . . .'

With the laying bare, however, went much destruction, and the vast, new transformations of the scenery of south Lancashire doubtless seemed to threaten a massive sweeping away of the old, familiar and settled. To scholarly people, the result was to make the past seem much more precious. The lurching instabilities of the new industrial world must have strengthened this feeling, to place a premium on the certainties and the fixed practices of the rural world of former days.

Perhaps it is not a total accident that the middle years of the century saw the burgeoning of the great Lancashire and Cheshire learned societies, which were primarily concerned with the recording of past antiquities, institutions, local lore and archaeology. The Chetham Society, which published its first annual volume of antiquarian matter in 1844, did so not long before the appearance of the first issue of the *Transactions* of the Historic Society of Lancashire and Cheshire (1849). The first volume of the archival and other edited works of the Record Society of the two counties was issued in 1878, and the Lancashire and Cheshire Antiquarian Society produced its first annual volume of *Transactions* in 1883. The reader will notice how regularly Lancashire and Cheshire are linked together in these titles, and this, too, is significant. Both the Historic Society, based on the Liverpool sub-region, and the Antiquarian Society, based largely on the Manchester area, catered for great centres of population which were themselves created by industry, and both fields of influence embraced the southerly county, where many professional people 'commuted' or retired.

Much of what follows is taken from the great body of scholarship assembled and published by these regional learned societies, and by specialist scholars working in the same tradition. If the bare condensations are inaccurate or badly presented, that is plainly the fault of the present author, although one should not overlook the intractable nature of much of the available published material. Many of the scholars concerned have shown a bias against the study of modern society, and the nineteenth-century antiquary was apt to associate the remoteness in time of a site or article with its enhanced significance. Accordingly, as Edward Baines charmingly put it, 'There is always a disposition in antiquaries to give a high date to their discoveries.'

ARCHAEOLOGY AND THE LANCASHIRE LANDSCAPE
Notwithstanding the time lavished upon Lancashire's more distant past, the fact is that archaeologically, if not in the antiquarian or

historical senses, the county is rather poor territory. Obviously, industry and urban spread have together done much damage, but another key to this somewhat negative conclusion is to be found in the county's geography and physical attributes. However, the former appearance of the Lancashire landscape is not immediately obvious to the present-day student. Well within historic times, lowland Lancashire was covered by forest or scrub, and fringed by meres and extensive coastal peatmosses in the northern and western Fylde, in the lower Ribble Valley and behind what is now Southport. These hindered easy access to the sea and its trade, especially where the mosses gave way to muddy salt-flats. There are certainly few traces of Neolithic or Bronze Age settlement over much of the plainland behind this peatmoss barrier, and there is evidence that even the Anglo-Saxon and Norse settlers were deflected by it.

Lancashire as a whole was thinly settled in pre-history, and the region was plainly inhospitable. Yet it seems that men were hunting in the area not very long after the retreat of the glaciers of the Ice Age, and the skeleton of an elk, found at Poulton-le-Fylde, together with two bone spear points and cut marks on the bone from other weapons, has been dated to about 10,000 BC. Forest was the dominant cover over much of the lowlands, and those of boulder clay, like the inner Fylde, Low Furness and the central Lancashire plain, seem to be archaeologically barren. The hills and moors of the northern limestone territory yield rather more evidence of settlement. Here crags and ridges (Warton, Castle Head near Grange, and Urswick in Furness) suggest Iron Age fortifications. Portfield near Whalley has yielded evidence of Neolithic and Bronze Age use, while Caster Cliff, Skelmore Heads near Ulverston and Portfield have been associated with the Iron Age. Urswick Stone Walls, the other Furness site mentioned, has produced evidence of Neolithic as well as Bronze and Iron Age occupation.

Each of these sites stands on or near fertile territory, especially the sweet limestone pasture of north Lancashire, and gold ornaments found at Portfield (which was accessible from the Ribble

Valley) may well have an Irish pedigree. What of the bare and rugged gritstone moors of east and central Lancashire, and the carboniferous uplands of Rossendale, Bowland and the Pennines? It has been suggested that a period of mild climate in the early Bronze Age encouraged movement on to the higher moors, which were almost certainly less peaty and forbidding than is now the case. Many discoveries of artefacts have been made on this higher ground, including arrowheads of Neolithic design and the 'factory axes' which were widely traded. On Winter Hill above Bolton, with its television masts, are cairns of Bronze Age type, and on Anglezarke Moor, only a few miles away, are the Pikestones, a chambered Neolithic long cairn. In Bleasdale, at a meeting point of moor and plain, there have been signs of a remarkable Bronze Age memorial, a ritual house-of-the-dead surrounded by a ditch and palisade. Special areas, like the middle Ribble Valley and Pilling Moss, have yielded Bronze Age finds.

ROMAN LANCASHIRE

The Romans can have found little to attract them commercially. Their arrival in AD 78–81 was certainly not followed by commercial exploitation, the subsequent occupation being almost purely military. Despite all that has been written about the Roman period in Lancashire, the occupation of the troops can have had little permanent effect on the county's history. There is, however, a shortage of certain information regarding it. The building of the permanent road network initiated by Agricola was completed about the time of the erection of Hadrian's Wall (AD 122–8), but *Deva* (Chester) was established as a legionary fort in AD 78, and subsequently *Mamucium* (Manchester) stood on the Chester–York road, York afterwards becoming the capital of northern (or Lower) Britain.

Accordingly Lancashire itself was not on any main route from the Wall, and the principal routes ran east of the Pennines. There is no evidence of a *colonia* of civilians (suggesting trading and craft development) even at Chester, although I. A. Richmond argued that groups of pensioned soldiers were settled in the Fylde and in

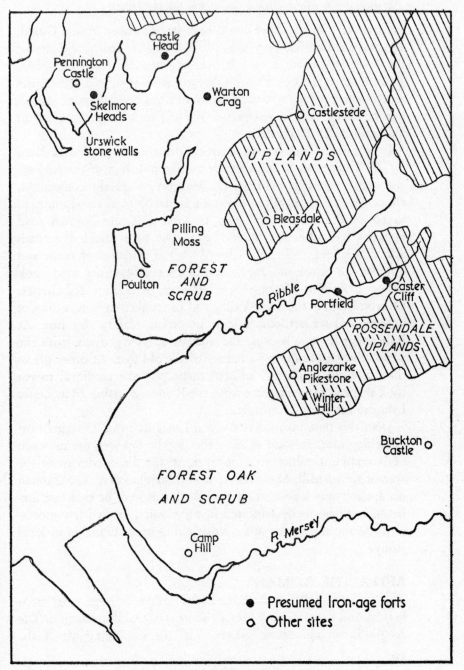

Fig 1 Prehistoric settlement in Lancashire

the Ribble Valley. These could have been a cheap Home Guard, and their settlement may indicate that security in the vicinity of the forts at Lancaster and Ribchester was far from complete. The tile kilns at Quernmoor suggest a well-organised occupation at Lancaster, where a Roman bathhouse has been revealed (1973), but the countryside in general is bereft of signs of private settlement in the form of villa remains.

Lancashire's Roman road network, described in passionate detail by W. Thompson Watkin, the Victorian historian of the subject, and more recently by Ivan D. Margary, is partly conjectural, although largely accepted from an archaeological standpoint. In so far as the reconstruction is a sound one, the Roman road network has influenced later routes. The forts which the roads joined together—Wigan, believed on the evidence of coins and pottery and of the mileages given in a second-century road book to be Coccium, Walton near Preston, Kirkham, Ribchester, Overborough in the Lune Valley and Lancaster—in some instances influenced later settlement, but in others plainly did not. At Ribchester the site became the nucleus of later growth, with the parish church occupying a corner of the old fort. At other places there was no continuity of settlement, and the medieval towns took shape at some distance from the Roman remains, Manchester being an interesting example.

Does this then mean that Roman Lancashire can be written off as lacking interest? Not at all; nobody who has seen the museum of Roman antiquities at Ribchester, or the discoveries from the area of Knott Mill, Manchester, would imagine that. The Roman occupation was a fascinating episode, but it may be that our forbears, conventionally educated in the classics, exalted it unnecessarily to the neglect of other equally important branches of local study.

AFTER THE ROMANS

The evidence relating to Roman Lancashire is largely archaeological, and there are few literary sources of real illumination. The Anglo-Saxon chroniclers likewise tell us something about the

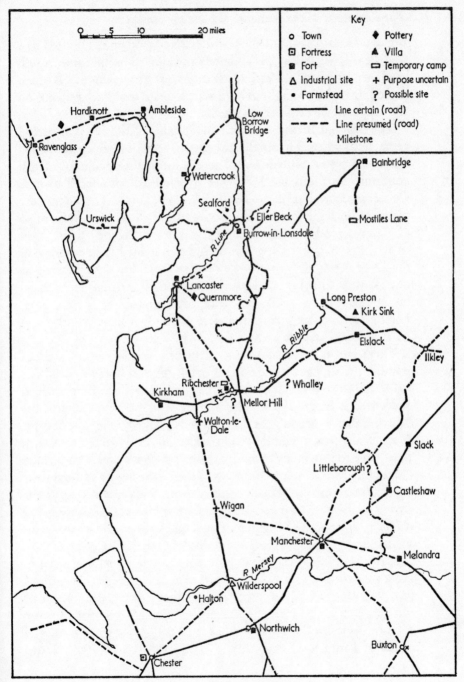

Key

○	Town	◆	Pottery
▣	Fortress	▲	Villa
▰	Fort	▱	Temporary camp
△	Industrial site	+	Purpose uncertain
•	Farmstead	?	Possible site
	Line certain (road)		
	Line presumed (road)		
×	Milestone		

Hardknott
Ambleside
Ravenglass
Low Borrow Bridge
Watercrook
Bainbridge
Sealford
Eller Beck
Mostiles Lane
Urswick
Burrow-in-Lonsdale
R. Lune
Lancaster
Quernmore
Long Preston
▲ Kirk Sink
R. Ribble
Elslack
Ilkley
Ribchester
? Whalley
Kirkham
? Mellor Hill
Walton-le-Dale
Slack
Littleborough?
Castleshaw
Wigan
Manchester
Melandra
R. Mersey
Wilderspool
Halton
Northwich
Buxton
Chester

B

Fig 2 Roman Lancashire

present county area, but the more material evidence is limited to a few hoards of coins; place-names provide us with some rough guidance only to successive invasions of Angles in the Roman period. It is now thought to be unwise to place too much reliance on the supposed dates of these names.

The original British or Celtic inhabitants of the Roman period remained scattered in small settlements, some of which remained unscathed by later invasions. There is interesting evidence of this continuity in the name *Eccles* and its variants, considered to be a Celtic degeneration of the Latin *ecclesia*, a church. The Lancashire places of Eccles, Eccleston and Eccleshill are all within a mile or so of Roman roads, showing that the natives established their places of worship at convenient points, and maintained their religion in the Dark Ages. However, their relative agricultural backwardness limited their influence and progress, and their techniques, pastoral in the main, may well have come from the middle Bronze Age. Fortunately, onslaughts by invaders must often have passed them by in this still remote area.

There is a theory that in the early fifth century some kind of popular revolt, against a house of petty kings in north-east Wales, led to the establishment of the 'lost kingdom of Teyrnllwg', which at its widest included Cheshire and most of Lancashire, until the Northumbrian victory at the battle of Chester in about 615. Meanwhile, from about 570, trickles of Anglian immigrants, following the main river valleys from the south and through the Pennines, are assumed to have established their *ingas* and then their *ingaham* settlements. (This, however, is only accepted theory; the dating of these place-names, and their possible order, is now being challenged generally.) Melling in the Lune Valley and also in south-west Lancashire, and Aldingham in Furness are examples.

A third wave of Anglian colonists is thought to have arrived in the seventh century, with settlements ending in *ing(a)ton* (Wennington, Whittington, Adlington). This century saw the dominance of the Anglian kingdom of Northumbria, which controlled large parts of northern England, and left its mark on the place-names of much of Lancashire, especially north of the Ribble, with forms such as Bolton (occurring several times) and Bootle. In the eighth century, however, the Midland kingdom of Mercia vied with Northumbria for leadership, and a different Anglian penetration from the west Midlands brought with it a recognisable change in dialect. This is demonstrated especially by a *ch* sound, as in Chadderton or Manchester. In north Lancashire the equivalent sound would be the hard *c*, as in Lancaster. However, there were no sharp divisions, and there are Northumbrian names south of the Ribble. The kingdoms of that age did not rule through all-embracing central organisation but through scattered tribal groups. Anglian settlement as a whole is indicated by endings or suffixes like -*bury*, -*ham*, or -*wick* or -*worth*. The reader should examine the county map to find how numerous these are.

In the ninth century, it was the turn of Wessex to act as leader of the English kingdoms, and by this time the Danish raids on the south and east coasts were already in progress. These gained momentum until the king of Mercia was driven into exile in 874, and the Danes accordingly overran most of the Midlands. They seem to have followed the path of the earlier Anglian–Mercian movement into south-east Lancashire, and Danish place-names occur principally in the Manchester area—names like Flixton and Urmston. *Flik* is a peculiarly Danish personal name, and *Urm* is also distinctively Danish. *Hulm*(e) is also a significant indicator of this kind. As has sometimes been remarked, Danes chose flattish places, 'just like home'.

THE NORSEMEN

The greatest Scandinavian invasion of Lancashire came from the sea, with the colonisation (from about 910) of the coastlands by Norsemen from Ireland, the Isle of Man and Scotland. Their settlement was performed fairly peacefully, judging by their tendency to farm near Anglian sites, and it seems that they, too, often went to country that was as nearly like their homeland as possible—the wooded hills of Furness especially attracted them, but had the additional virtue of being vacant. Generally, their explorers stayed in the coastal areas lying between the lowering

Lakeland hills and the Welsh mountains, and accordingly their place-names—like Scarisbrick, Formby, Altcar, Ainsdale, Birkdale, Warbreck and Kellamergh—are in former mossland, inferior damp territory which the Angles seem to have left alone. Nor did they push the former British out; Halsall, in the middle of this territory, is a British name.

However, many names of the type quoted could be either Danish or Norwegian. But the distinguished etymologist Eilert Ekwall showed that certain names contain elements which are distinctively Norwegian: *brekka* as in Norbreck, *skáli* as in Brinscall or Scales, or *slakki* as in Nettleslack or Ashlack. Such names reveal other vital morsels of information, for example the use of the Irish form *airge* (Old Norse, *erg*) as in Goosnargh, which also contains the Irish personal name *Gusan*. The scholarly detective is thus not satisfied with the vague heading 'Scandinavian'. He can show that these were Norway-originated settlers who came, as we have seen, from Ireland or via the Isle of Man.

Moreover, the evidence of settlement, provided by place-names, is much more rich than these few comments would imply, and it runs to many thousands of minor names of farm, clearing or hamlet, like the *thveit* or 'thwaite' cleared by the Norseman's iron axe. But here we must be even more careful, for much in the Norse language passed into dialect—an indicator of its vast influence—and some names of this kind, especially of field or farm, may have been given by later inhabitants. Hence, already established names, like the Anglian Whittingham, received for a time a Norse inflection and became *Whitingeheim*. Small hills and streams which lacked names may have been given Norse ones by people who were not the original Scandinavian settlers.

How far did this influence extend? The place-names Brinscall, near Chorley, or Anglezarke in the same area, suggest the eastern limit of their intensive colonisation; relatively few Scandinavian names occur in east Lancashire, although, as Ekwall showed, the Danes had some influence there, and a few Norwegians may have settled the *booths* of that area. In west Lancashire as a whole, Norse influence was abiding. Their administration is reflected in the name

Thingwall, the *thing* being an assembly of a tribe or district. They influenced not only speech, but the genetic characteristics and the social organisation of the region, and they left, in a lead-lined chest by the banks of the Ribble at Cuerdale, the largest Viking silver treasure outside Russia, found by workmen in 1840. Their art has left its traces in the wheelheaded stone crosses at Halton, Lancaster, Urswick and Winwick, with their characteristic snake and dragon decorations, and in the hogback tomb at Heysham (about AD 1000), which seem to bring pagan and Christian symbols side by side.

These survivals indicate that the Norsemen, like the Anglians, were proto-Christians. St Patrick's chapel at Heysham may have been built by the Anglians considerably earlier than AD 1000. Generally, the evidence for Christianisation in Lancashire is rather thin, and rests partly on the place-names we have mentioned, Eccles and Eccleston. Domesday Book, as we shall see, contains numerous references to churches in Lancashire, and there can be little doubt that many of these were of pre-Conquest origin.

Although the confused political history of this age can have had only indirect significance for its world of pioneering colonists and lonely settlements, the struggle against the Danes and Norsemen and the Mercian enemies of Wessex carried on by the successors of King Alfred, which reached its climax at the battle of Brunanburgh in 937, forced the movement of the boundary of Northumbria to the Ribble. The land between the Ribble and the Mersey became a royal domain, separate from Mercia, and remained so until after the Conquest. This accident has affected our knowledge of the county's early history.

WHAT TO READ

First of all, general surveys: Mr J. J. Bagley's *History of Lancashire with Maps and Pictures* (first published in 1956, and now available in revised form), will help the reader of this book in many parallel details, particularly in its fine summaries of pre-modern history. The introductory sections in Freeman, Rodgers and Kinvig, *Lancashire, Cheshire and the Isle of Man* (1966) give a most useful outline of the early settlement of Lancashire in relation to geography. Mr R. Millward's *Lancashire: An Illustrated Essay on the History of the Landscape* (1955) is a most stimulating survey.

Having looked at the great pioneering works like Baines, the reader will wish to know what the findings of recent scholarship have to say about early Lancashire history. He will find some interesting articles in the *Transactions of the Lancashire and Cheshire Antiquarian Society*, notably Dr J. D. Bu'lock (on the Pikestones) in vol 68 for 1958, and Mr J. Forde-Johnston (on Iron Age hill forts) in vol 72 for 1962. A wealth of critical scholarship is represented by the presidential address to the Society by Dr J. A. Petch on Roman Lancashire, in vol 69 for 1959. But before reading this, the reader should fortify himself by studying I. A. Richmond, *Roman Britain* (in the Pelican series), and also the Ordnance Survey Map of Roman Britain (3rd ed, 1956). Volume 2 of Ivan D. Margary's *Roman Roads in Britain* (1957), which includes Lancashire, will do something to prevent the student being swept away by the sometimes misguided enthusiasm of W. T. Watkin, *Roman Lancashire* (1883). Dr D. C. A. Shotter's Dalesman handbook *Romans in Lancashire* (1973) is an excellent up-to-date guide. That later history which makes much use of place-names is well catered for by E. Ekwall, *The Place-Names of Lancashire* (Chetham Society, vol 81, 1922), but there is also an important article by F. T. Wainwright in the *Transactions of the Historic Society of Lancashire and Cheshire* (vol 93, 1941), 'The Anglian Settlement of Lancashire', and another one by the same authority, 'The Scandinavians in Lancashire', in the *Transactions of the Lancashire and Cheshire Antiquarian Society* (vol 58, 1945–6).

Chapter 2   DOMESDAY AND
MEDIEVAL LANCASHIRE

THE Lancashire of William the Conqueror is covered only very incompletely in Domesday Book (1086), and it was in any case too poor and thinly peopled to offer much encouragement to the invader. Its rise to full status as a county division was delayed until the late twelfth century, and accordingly the Domesday record treats its northern hundreds, those beyond the Ribble, as an appendage of Yorkshire, including them with vills in south Westmorland and south Cumberland. South Lancashire *inter Ripam et Mersham*—'between the Ribble and the Mersey'—is given as a sort of appendix to the much more richly detailed account of Cheshire.

What is the picture of Conquest Lancashire which emerges? The marshes east of the Wyre estuary, and the marshy country behind present-day Southport, remained thinly settled in the extreme. But in the drier lands of the central Fylde, in the lower foothills and valleys around Morecambe Bay, in the countryside between present-day St Helens and Wigan, and along the Ribble Valley, there were numerous scattered vills and settlements. Here, as already mentioned, the original Anglo-Saxon settlers had been joined by Norsemen, and these areas must have contained closely and regularly cultivated stretches of ploughland. The place-names of Domesday Book are still well represented in south-west Lancashire (West Derby Hundred), and they ring in the ears of the modern Liverpudlian: *Alretune* (Allerton), *Spec* (Speke), *Uluentune* (Woolton), *Hitune* (Huyton), *Sextone* (Sefton). Here the reader should not be misled, for there were few substantial towns or even villages in the county, and only Penwortham, near Preston, is given as containing burgesses. Perhaps the reference is really to Preston itself. There was little to be seen in the central area of modern Liverpool, and Manchester, the former *Mamucium*, is mentioned in passing as having a church.

There were very few settlements in the county above the 500ft contour and, as far as we know, none at all above 800ft. Even central and south-west Lancashire were quite heavily wooded, and those woods were wild enough to contain deer, who seem to have been kept from the crops by deer-heys or enclosures; the place-name *hey* (OE, hedge) still occurs in Lancashire, like Bryan Hey on the moor above Bolton. On the other hand, there are only four references to *waste* in the whole of the 1086 survey, therefore it may be that very little land had been left untended and allowed to go back to undergrowth, and so, perhaps, few villages had been looted or burnt.

MEDIEVAL AGRICULTURE

We know very little about the agriculture of this age; place-names from Anglian or Norse times show that barley, wheat, rye and oats (especially, perhaps, the latter) were known, yet, extraordinarily, the places Barley and Wheatley are high up in the Forest of Pendle. The penetration of the empty Bowland foothills took place long after Domesday, not so much by the creation of villages as through settlement by 'squatter' farmers. In other areas, like High Furness, there was also scattered settlement, in that case of Norse origin, and the pattern of isolated farms or hamlets, linked by scattered tracks, remains to this day. Much of this agriculture was pastoral, and in Rossendale and Bowland, influential families or monasteries established cattle farms in the later Middle Ages, or ran sheep on the moors. Hence the *folds* of southeast Lancashire appeared. The *booths*, associated with these cattle farmers, may earlier have had Scandinavian settlers.

The larger vills or settlements in plainland Lancashire, large enough to take 'nucleated' form and situated outside the mosslands or coastal marshes, probably farmed in small 'town' or common fields, made by breaking into new ground periodically. These fields were used for pasture as well as ploughland, and sometimes very small hamlets, like Orgrave in Furness, had lands in a common field, *in campo*. The basic crop grown was almost certainly oats, a spring-sown cereal well suited to the Lancashire climate. Spring sowing has the advantage that it does away with the need for a summer fallow, when the land is given a rest, and since there are no seeds in the ground in winter, cattle can be turned on to these fields to fertilise them. Above all, there was no need to group people's arable or other strips into two or three large fields of the traditionally pictured kind, and follow a large-scale, clumsy rotation every year, because this type of farming allowed for much more variety of crop and holding. As in the sixteenth-century illustrated plan of Lytham (Fig 3), the arable and other fields of a township—which might in fact contain several different crops— might be scattered around it in heys or enclosures. Such an arrange- ment was *flexible*, so that wheat could be grown in small separate closes, as is suggested by the names *wheatcroft* and *wheathey*.

The field system, sometimes called 'Celtic' but probably origina- ted by Anglian settlers from Northumbria in many localities, plainly allowed for individual enterprise. Free tenants, individualist cultivators or small owners, became fairly numerous in medieval Lancashire, and the small fields could in any case be taken over or split by enterprising farmers. Hence, Lancashire was an 'enclosed' county, in its plainland areas, long before parliamentary procedure enabled big landlords to divide up the countryside in the eighteenth century.

Much of the countryside, however, was in a wild state, and the systematic clearing of wood and scrubland began about the middle of the twelfth century. Some part in this process was played by the monastic houses, of which Furness, Whalley and Cockersand were major foundations. Furness Abbey was already developing its agriculture in that century (it had been founded in 1127), and had granges or farming settlements scattered about the fertile lowland of the Furness peninsula. Whalley Abbey, like that of Furness, was interested in sheep farming. But the real indicators of agricultural

25

development and growing individual wealth are twofold: the establishment of markets and fairs, and the building of churches, which would have been impossible without material resources.

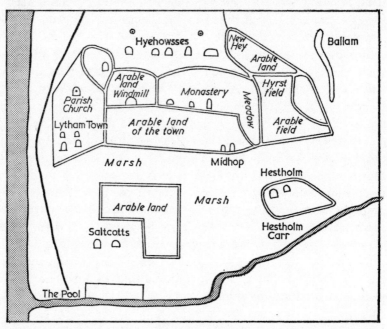

Fig 3   Sixteenth-century 'town' fields at Lytham (from a plan at the Lancashire Record Office)

MARKETS AND FAIRS

Thirteenth-century Lancashire saw a marked development of both markets and fairs. Although no Lancashire mart is mentioned in Domesday Book, it is highly probable that Preston, with its excellent position at the head of an estuary and at an intersection of main routes, was already known as a market centre. Its privilege of holding an annual fair was confirmed by King John in 1199, and in the same year a market at Warton in north Lancashire was granted to one Gilbert Fitz Reinfred. The *Quo Warranto* proceedings of nearly a century later show that other places had markets and fairs already well established—Clitheroe, Cartmel, Dalton-in-

Furness and Hornby. Indeed, by the end of King John's reign (1216) there were at least ten market and fair centres, out of which no fewer than seven were north of the Ribble; these included Lancaster in the north and Liverpool and Warrington in the southwest.

The 'new' market centres of this age are a bewildering mixture of what were to become the important towns of the modern period, and places which are still villages. Hence, during the thirteenth century, Salford, Rochdale, Wigan and Bolton all received or acquired the right to have markets and fairs, side by side with North Meols (later Southport) and Walton-le-Dale. In the reign of Edward I, Burnley and Ormskirk were added to the list, together with Charnock Richard, Croston, Arkholme and Ulverston. By that time, the balance had been tipped very much in favour of south Lancashire, and by 1307 there were at least twice as many market towns south of the Ribble as there were north of it. Manchester's fair charter was confirmed in 1227.

Thus, the surface pattern of modern Lancashire seems to be taking shape. But this is really misleading. The new markets were centres of small islands of activity, in which the inhabitants would be aware mainly of their own limited area, parish or manor.

THE BUILDING OF CHURCHES

The appearance of churches is also a good guide to growing population and is some measure of modest economic development. References in Domesday Book indicate that there were then (1086) eighteen churches in what is now Lancashire, and to these we may, in the light of varying evidence, add churches at Heysham, Lytham, Eccleston, Melling, Bolton-le-Sands and Croston. Melling and Bolton-le-Sands, for example, have pieces of pre-Norman Christian crosses. On the whole, then, twenty-four or more of our Lancashire churches were founded in or before Anglo-Saxon times.

By 1291, the number had more than doubled, at least thirty-two having been added. Yet, the surprising fact is that after this great burst of church or chapel building, only three new parishes were

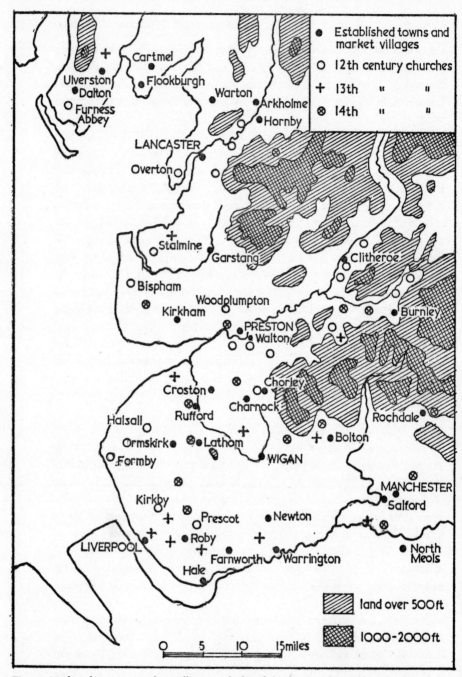

Fig 4 Medieval towns, market villages and churches in Lancashire. This diagram is not exhaustive, and shows some tendencies outside the towns (eg in the Ribble Valley).

created during the following 300 years. Most of the medieval parishes were large ones—the parish of Whalley was 180 square miles in area, and that of Lancaster 110 square miles—and so more than 20 chapels-of-ease appeared by the end of the twelfth century, and 38 by the beginning of the fourteenth. These were designed to help people in remote or swampy territory to worship at a reasonably convenient place, and so their appearance is not a direct guide to population. There was a noteworthy growth of these chapels in north and north-east Lancashire, and these areas, as in the case of markets and fairs, seemed to lead the way at first; in fact, however, some of this growth is attributable to the abbeys of Furness and Whalley and their interest in serving local populations. Church building, for reasons which will become clear, was slow in the later fourteenth century.

In the fifteenth and sixteenth centuries there was a great expansion of church and chapel building in south and south-east Lancashire, especially new chapels, and some of this building, by zealous individuals rather than monastic houses, may reflect a slow growth of the textile industries and small wealth connected therewith.

THE EMERGENCE OF THE COUNTY

The church played a key part in social life and local administration. But, since the consciousness of most people cannot have extended beyond local confines, most of the population must have been totally unaware of the first steps towards the formation of the county of Lancashire, which were taken before the end of the twelfth century.

The Domesday surveyors, as has been noted, saw the northern part of Lancashire as belonging to Yorkshire, and the part south of the Ribble to Cheshire. However, the first vital step towards the creation of Lancashire was effected when the Conqueror gave his eminent helper, Roger of Poitou, the land between Ribble and Mersey and *also* that territory later known as Lonsdale Hundred, ie the land around Morecambe Bay, together with the town of Lancaster. Roger made Lancaster his strategic centre, because it could control the vital coast route from Scotland, and the oversands area of Furness made a logical part of the same defence system. Furness thus became part of the later Lancashire. These northern territories became known as *Lancastre*. In 1102 Roger forfeited his lands in the honour of Lancaster to the Crown, but the two areas (south-west Lancashire and Lonsdale) remained an entity. They were not finally recognised as parts of a separate shire until 1182, when the exchequer clerks began to refer to this distant region as *Lancastra*, the lands between the Mersey and the Duddon. The expression 'county of Lancaster' was used as early as 1168. In this way the strangely-shaped area, with its remote county town, arrived late in the list of English shires.

In 1189, Richard I granted the honour of Lancaster to his brother John, Count of Mortain and later the King John of dubious memory. This man played some part in building up the administrative identity of the area by reaffirming the privileges of Lancaster and Preston, and by granting a charter to the still embryonic borough of Liverpool.

Meanwhile, a form of county administration, much subject to the struggles among the supporters and enemies of royal factions, had developed during this period. The responsibility for the preservation of the peace within the county rested firstly upon the sheriff, and secondly upon the bailiffs of the hundreds into which the county had by this time become divided, such main divisions having been foreshadowed by Domesday. Courts were held by the sheriff for the whole county, and the bailiffs presided at special sessions for individual hundreds, the officers at both levels dealing with felonies and crimes of violence.

The *earl* of Lancaster, however, was an individual to whom these officers owed allegiance, and the earldom was in effect created by Edmund (d 1296), the youngest son of Henry III. Its privileges included the possession of the lordship *and* the right to appoint the sheriff; hence, when the earl became the king's enemy, as happened in the time of the notorious Thomas of Lancaster, Edmund's eldest son, the county officers suffered from divided loyalties. The early fourteenth century brought surges of private warfare between county gentry factions, unhappy tendencies which did not really cease until the accession of the Tudors. The supporters of a given faction might be protected from the legal consequences of the worst crimes; the same period brought, in addition, a frightful invasion of the county by the Scots under Robert the Bruce (1322), when the pillaging invaders reached as far as Chorley.

THE COUNTY PALATINE

'The Queen—the Duke of Lancaster'; this toast is today a part of Lancashire life. The Dukedom of Lancaster was created in 1351, as a reward for the loyalty to Edward III of Henry of Lancaster, the son of the notorious Thomas. King Edward also gave Henry a momentous privilege, that of wielding *palatinate* powers. This really meant that Duke Henry could run Lancashire as though it were a separate kingdom, with 'palace' (palatine) authority. He could set up his own chancery, or secretariat, and appoint his own justices for his own criminal or civil courts, so that legal business in Lancaster or Preston could be carried on quite independently of London. He did not, however, levy taxation independently of the Crown, and Edward III insisted that national taxation should be paid directly to him, even from the county area. Lancashire was still obliged to send its two county MPs (or knights of the shire), and its eight borough members (two each for Preston, Lancaster, Wigan and Liverpool) to parliament.

The dukedom, and the palatine powers, lapsed with Duke Henry's death in 1361. Sixteen years later, the famous John of Gaunt was enabled to unite both in his own person, and in 1399 King Henry IV took both title and powers into what was to be the permanent custody of the Crown. The Duchy of Lancaster became not a separate state, but a part of the British Crown possessions and of the constitution. Its separate courts continued; and its office and council, after removal to London, administered Henry's duchy estates all over England as well as in Lancashire. Although the duchy was shorn of most of its powers by the Judicature Act of 1873, the Chancellor of the Duchy, a political office-holder, still appoints judges and magistrates for the county.

These constitutional niceties have meant little to the ordinary Lancastrian. During the fourteenth century, when they were being clarified, the people of the county suffered unusual hardship and privation. Starvation and pestilence (1314–16) was accompanied by the Banastre Revolt, when Sir Adam Banastre of Shevington (1315) led a rising against the Hollands, powerful hangers-on of Thomas of Lancaster. The local civil war continued in stages, and the county was still in turmoil when the Scots arrived. As the late Dr Tupling remarked of this period: 'The forests of Bleasdale, Wyresdale and Fulwood, the chases of Blackburnshire, the parks of Myerscough, Toxteth, Healey, Pimbo, Linhale, Musbury . . . were spoiled of their deer and timber, and the vaccaries of Rossendale, Pendle and Trawden were depleted of their livestock.' The Inquisition of the Ninth in 1341 revealed widespread poverty and distress, and the general restlessness remained until the catastrophe of the Black Death in 1349–51. It is little wonder that church building slowed down appreciably in the later fourteenth century.

SIGNS OF ECONOMIC LIFE

Yet there were stirrings of commercial and industrial development which cannot have been entirely submerged even during these troubled times. The textile industries were in being, and there were fulling mills on the Irk at Manchester and at Colne and Burnley towards the end of the thirteenth century, just as there was a dyer at work in Ancoats in the middle of that century. Towards its final decades, coal was being worked at Colne, Trawden and Bolton, probably in shallow surface workings. The right to mine iron ore was granted to Furness Abbey in the thirteenth and late fourteenth centuries.

There are other indicators of economic life; there was a Preston Gild celebration as early as 1329, and that town had a cattle fair or market even in the previous century. There was bridge-building, and even paving of streets, in fourteenth-century Liverpool and Wigan. In the far north of the county, Piel Castle stood guard over vessels at the anchorage near Furness Abbey. It has been suggested that this somewhat mysterious landmark in oversands Lancashire was as much a woollen warehouse as a military stronghold, and it is known that the abbots brought in corn from Ireland and smuggled wool out of the country to Flanders. It is hard to believe that other havens on the Lancashire coast did not share in such trade.

WHAT TO READ

The best and most illuminating source on Domesday Lancashire is H. C. Darby and I. S. Maxwell (eds), *The Domesday Geography of Northern England* (1962), especially Chap 7, by I. B. Terrett, which deals with Lancashire. There is also a useful survey in vol 1 of the *Victoria County History for Lancashire*, pp 269–90. Volume 2 of the same work contains a useful though very old-fashioned account of the economic and social history of the county, including that of the Middle Ages, and the same volume gives an account of the monastic houses of the period.

Important articles on the common fields of Lancashire (by Youd, Singleton, Cunliffe Shaw and Tyrer) are contained in the *Transactions of the Historic Society for Lancashire and Cheshire*, vols 113, 114 and 115. Markets and fairs are dealt with by the late Dr G. H. Tupling in the *Transactions of the Antiquarian Society*, vols 49, 50, 51 and 58, and Lancashire churches are surveyed by the same author in vols 60 and 67. Dr Tupling's Chetham Society volume, *Lancashire in the Time of Edward II* (vol 1, 3rd series), contains much valuable background matter on the upheavals of the fourteenth century, and Sir Robert Somerville's major work, *The History of the Duchy of Lancaster*, vol 1, is supplemented by an article on the same subject in the Historic Society's vol 103.

Chapter 3   TUDOR AND STUART
LANCASHIRE: WEALTH,
POVERTY, POPULATION
AND RELIGION

THE AGRICULTURAL SCENE

UNTIL well into the seventeenth century,
Lancashire's basic wealth lay in its agriculture. Largely agrarian
parts of the county, like south-west Lancashire, were the most
·promising territories from the tax-gatherer's point of view, and
the southern and south-eastern parts (Salford Hundred) had not
then become areas of industrial advance to anything like the
extent of later centuries.

However, much of the county was moorland or mossland,
although some agricultural expansion may well have taken place
in late medieval and Tudor times. Thanks to the work of Professor
H. B. Rodgers, a plan of its probable agricultural regions of that
age has been prepared from the Final Concords (ie feet of fines or
agreements relating to land, available in the Lancashire and Cheshire Record Society, vols 39, 46, 50 and 60). As Fig 5 shows, there
were two great regions of essentially pastoral farming, Bowland
(and Lonsdale) and Rossendale. Here 'waste' may have accounted
for between 45 and 60 per cent of the total areas, and there was
comparatively little ploughland but a fair amount of meadow in
the valleys. A large part of the Fylde was also given over to pasture,
but a wide band of arable territory occupied the inner Lancashire
plain and part of the Ribble Valley. This arable group of sub-
regions seems to have been the least affected by poverty at the time

of the hearth tax of 1664. In this central arable belt and perhaps elsewhere in the plain, John Leland saw 'closes all the way'—that is to say a patchwork of hedges of *heys*—in his visit about 1540. There were common pastures in or near villages, but large arable open fields were rare, and it may be that some of the latter had disappeared, as a result of Tudor or earlier enclosures.

In south-west Lancashire, pasture land exceeded the probable arable area, and much of its wealth must have lain in its cattle. Until the 1530s, meanwhile, cattle had been more numerous than any other kind of livestock in Rossendale, which had contained medieval vaccaries (cattle farms). By this time, however, sheep were becoming serious rivals, although their numbers should not be exaggerated. For example, Whalley Abbey in 1536 took 107 stones of wool in tithes from eleven major chapelries of east Lancashire, including Rossendale, Burnley and Pendle. If we allow 2 to 3lb to a fleece, and then multiply by ten, the number of immediately productive abbey sheep cannot have greatly exceeded 7,000. Perhaps an east Lancashire sheep population of two to three times that number will not be far from the mark. This modest total is supported by the probate inventories of the later Tudor period (lists of possessions deposited with yeoman and other wills). These indicate that it was unusual for a yeoman or husbandman to have many more than 50 sheep. A few east Lancashire land-owners and yeomen had considerably more, like the Shuttleworths (about 1590), who kept flocks totalling between 1,000 and 1,500 on their Burnley estates. This was plainly exceptional.

The sheep, scant though their production of wool might have been, were instrumental in providing the raw material for the most important sections of Lancashire's rising textile industry, and it is not surprising that in the exacting and agriculturally poor environment of the Lancashire moors, with their great stretches of dark green or russet 'waste' and acid soils, the inhabitants turned more and more to spinning or weaving woollens. The wool was there, the water was soft, and there was time for the work.

The probate inventories show that flax and hemp were grown in west Lancashire, and that a linen industry was well established by

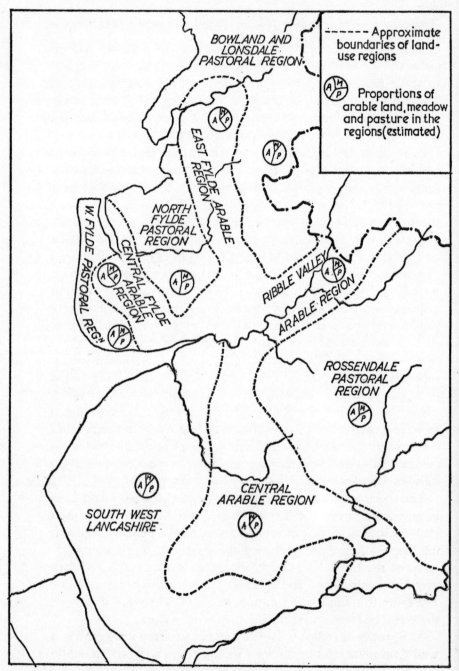

Fig 5   Land use regions in the Tudor period from Final Concords (by courtesy of Professor H. B. Rodgers)

Tudor times. Not surprisingly, the plainland farmers had markedly fewer sheep than the hill yeomen, and there was a greater interest in cattle than in the moorland east, with an average herd of ten to twelve beasts. There is also stronger evidence of cereal growing. Hence Thomas Gill, of Bickerstaff, Ormskirk (1593), had quantities of oats, barley and rye, while Humphrey Davis of Barton-on-Irwell (1594) grew barley and oats, and Robert Molyneaux of Sefton (1617) grew barley, rye, oats, beans and peas as well as wheat. It should be borne in mind, however, that much of west and south-west Lancashire was undrained, unreclaimed mossland. Few great landowners could yet undertake improvement.

LANDOWNERS AND CATHOLICISM

Lancashire remained a remote county, well away from the direct control of central governments, with its nearest border 150 slow and miry miles from London. The powerful Stanley family, Earls of Derby, were near-monarchs in this territory, and they acted as a formidable and sometimes uncertain link with the throne. This intermediary function was not an easy one, for the Dissolution of the Monasteries (1536) did little to weaken Lancashire Catholicism, and many of its great landowners continued to adhere to the old faith, including the Blundells of Crosby, the Heskeths of Rufford and Aughton, the Norris family of Speke, and the Molyneaux and Assheton families. West Lancashire, where most of the leading Catholics lived, was itself a remote microcosm of muddy lanes and marshland, in which seminary priests could move without real danger. The old faith left a deep impression on the country people, and it is relevant to ask why.

Although Lancashire's monastic houses had been far from outstandingly wealthy or powerful—Furness was the largest, richest and most important, as its ruins still testify—their vitality, splendour and demonstrative charity commended them profoundly to local peasants, and the suppression of 1536 was followed by the Pilgrimage of Grace, a rebellion of the northern countryside which drew several thousand active supporters in north Lancashire alone. In the south-western plain country of the county such support was much less in evidence, although there were several small monastic houses (Burscough, Holland, Penwortham, Preston and Warrington) in that area or near it. But the more splendid abbey of Whalley, run like some hospitable country mansion, left an abiding influence in the form of large numbers of Catholic recusants in the Ribble Valley, led by the Towneley, Southworth and Sherburne families, who gave much cause for concern to Elizabeth's government. On the other hand, rural Lancashire was in any case profoundly conservative, not to say backward and superstitious, and there is no simple cause and effect. Anglicanism, let alone its puritanical extremes, stood little chance in the deep fastnesses of the Fylde or the moss and mere country of the south-west.

The Catholic influence was later to reappear in the Jacobite groups of the late seventeenth and early eighteenth centuries. Ironically, it was often the Catholic landowner, or one with Catholic connections, who acquired former monastic lands, and accordingly there was no clear creation of a 'new' Anglican-biased landowner class by such means. The Earls of Derby, who certainly gained monastic territories, nevertheless took an opportunistic but fairly liberal view of Catholic neighbours, applying measures against recusants only when strategically necessary. There were a few speculators from outside the county, but they had little effect on the main course of events.

The larger landowners nevertheless played an important part in the Lancashire history of the next three centuries. So did another group of land-occupiers, the yeoman-clothiers.

TEXTILES, TOWNS AND PURITANISM

As we have seen, textiles and agriculture were closely connected. In the sixteenth century, the woollen industry was slowly losing its medieval form. The majority of woollen producers were yeomen or husbandmen who worked at home with the help of their families, owning a loom and a spinning wheel or two. Such men bought or grew small quantities of the very coarse local wool, and were self-employed, that is to say, they were free to sell their cloth or yarn to the best buyer. But, as time went on, they might be employed by clothiers who supplied them with raw material and who expected to receive the woven cloth in return. Linen was also woven.

In the sixteenth century, Lancashire woollen cloths went by the names of rugs, friezes, kerseys and cottons (the latter being woollen cloths despite the title). These found markets in Yorkshire, the Midlands, Bristol and Southampton, and were exported to France in the middle years of the century. In addition, there was a growing connection with London which was to prove itself of the greatest importance in the county's religious and social history.

The quantities of Lancashire cloth exported were not great, nor were there any very rich clothiers in the county before the end of Elizabeth's reign. But there were a few well-organised producers, nearly all of them in the Manchester-Salford locality, who employed as many as a dozen men in a textile workshop. In addition, dyeing, fulling (the matting of the cloth web by water-powered wooden hammers in bracken ash or soft soap), and the shearing of the nap, or rough surface of the cloth, came to be more often specialised occupations in the later years of the century, especially in the Manchester district. Merchants, too, congregated in the latter. Likewise, market towns like Bolton, Bury, Rochdale, Blackburn and Colne, all tiny enough places in themselves, began to specialise in textiles, as places where wool and yarn could be stored and bought, where cloth could be taken for fulling, dyeing and bleaching and shearing, or where it could be sold to dealers.

One important characteristic of these towns was that they were *free* or non-corporate; anybody could trade or produce in them. The corporate towns, which were governed by exclusive bodies of gildsmen and office-holders, were Wigan, Preston, Liverpool, and the rather remote little port of Lancaster. Liverpool was run by an enterprising corporation of merchants, but Wigan and Preston, the latter being an important market and linen centre, tended to mark time. Preston tried to control the country linen producers in its own area, but failed to stop the development of a rural, unregulated linen industry, this in the late seventeenth century. The other corporate towns regulated their internal craftsmen and traders. Significantly, free and open Manchester grew far faster than any of them. Apart from this, Lancashire towns (as everywhere) have grown with the aid of a great variety of stimuli, by very complex processes, and, despite corporate control, Liverpool and Preston were to become vastly important places.

Moreover, much of Lancashire's woollen manufacture was pursued in the countryside, especially near the towns themselves, and the weavers who supplied cloth for finishing often worked just outside the town, as in the case of Manchester. The country 'fed' the towns in this way. Meanwhile, the textile industries became more highly organised. The old traditional woollen 'cottons' gave way to 'bays', which had warp-threads of combed or long-staple wool, and south Lancashire itself became more and more involved in the production of smallwares, ie ribbons, garters and haberdashery. Most important of all, the use of cotton fibre, the vegetable kind, became widespread through the manufacture of fustian, a mixture of cotton weft and linen warp, and this fabric was made in southern central Lancashire, between Manchester and Blackburn. The cotton industry arose from this earlier one.

These manufactures, then, were largely rural, and were increasingly controlled by clothiers, often men of yeoman background, who organised production in the farms and cottages, who collected together the raw wool or cotton, and who gave out work and paid for it by the piece. But the wealthier merchants and clothiers naturally congregated in the towns, especially in the growing centre of Manchester-Salford, which had rather over 1,000 hearths, or about 5,000 population, in 1664. No other Lancashire town could match such affluence, although Preston had nine persons with eight hearths or over, and in that town county society was building its 'town' houses. Lancaster, too, had some rich people. The most important places, in order of size, were Manchester-Salford, Wigan, Bolton, Preston and Warrington, with Liverpool, Blackburn, Lancaster and Rochdale all under the 300 houses mark. These towns consisted, at most, of three or four main streets with a scattering of warehouses, shops and public buildings.

Even in the tiny town of Bury, however, John Brooke, a yeoman, had eight hearths, and his probate inventory of October 1676 shows him as possessing at least nine main rooms to his house, with a Red Chamber, a Green Chamber and a Brown Chamber. Against this, Richard Lomax sr, also of Bury (1676) had a mere four hearths but left movable goods to the then large sum of £2,198. Other yeomen and small merchants were plainly filling their houses with a variety of goods. Yet the leading figures in these towns were often dedicated puritans, as self-confident and dogmatic as they were experienced in commerce, organisation and accounting.

It is wrong, however, to assume that wealth and commercial enterprise alone lay behind puritanism. It was a feature of life in market towns and villages through the south and east of the county, and its gospel of hard work and high-mindedness was spread to substantial urban audiences. On the other hand, the established church was weak in Lancashire; beset by adherents of the old Catholic faith on the one hand, and the passionate puritans of the towns and the textile villages on the other, it became weaker in its effect as the population of the early seventeenth-century textile villages and districts became greater. The clergy of the largest parishes in these areas by degrees lost control of their flocks, and new chapels were built and opened, to fall under puritan influence. The leadership of Lancashire town puritanism came from Manchester, and Manchester in turn drew strength from its trade-induced links with London puritan example. Meanwhile, Lancashire's Catholicism acted as a profound stimulus to the puritan opposition, who attacked papist influence with passionate zeal. The established clergy not only lacked this fire, but were often less well educated.

THE CIVIL WAR

Lancashire leaders, then, took predictable sides in the Civil War. The towns of the south-east were for Parliament, and the country gentry, on the whole, were for the King. The story of the marches, counter-marches, sieges and battles has been told many times;

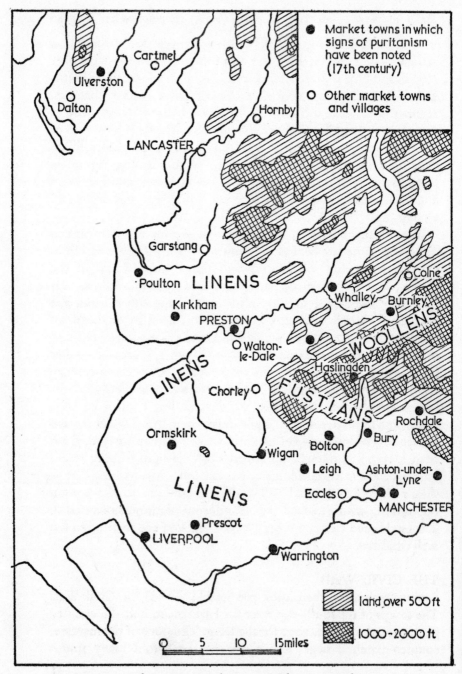

Fig 6 Lancashire puritan market towns in the seventeenth century

what is certain is that the great mass of the Lancashire population took neither side. Manchester stood and resisted stoutly for Parliament (1642) and Bolton was subject to a massacre (1644) by the troops of the Earl of Derby, representing the royal cause. In 1646 the whole of Lancashire was subject to Presbyterian organisation, which replaced the Anglican church, and this experiment had long-term effects which far outlasted its few years of official existence.

The Civil War also released enthusiasm for a mass of dissenting sects. Indeed, the great founder of Quakerism, George Fox, flexed his campaigning muscles against Presbyterian and other priests in the extreme north of the county in 1652, and in a few years Furness and north Lancashire became a centre of Quakerism. Swarthmoor Hall has a special place in Quaker history. The puritan tradition was carried forward as the Lancashire Presbyterians allied themselves with congregationalism. But the other 'old dissenters', Quakers, Baptists and Unitarians, later lost much of their fire and became somewhat exclusive—and successful in business, or distinguished in education.

The Roman Catholic tradition of the western countryside remained deeply rooted also, and Lancashire was to remain a stronghold of Jacobite or pro-Stuart sentiment a century after the Civil War. But a probable large majority of Lancashire people remained suspicious of change and deeply superstitious. The age of the Stuarts was also that of the witches of Pendle.

PLAGUE, POVERTY AND POPULATION

Although there were plenty of indications of industrial activity in seventeenth-century Lancashire—in a variety of small trades, coal and metal-working as well as in textiles—we should bear in mind that its wealth was very thinly spread. It has long been a commonplace that there can be no great surge forward of industrialisation without a similar development of agriculture or food supplies, and the possessions and stores of goods listed in the inventories of husbandmen suggest that they were producing only small supplies for the market. A few large landowners may by this time have

43

Fig 7 Tockholes Chapel, near Darwen, centre of nonconformity

produced food on a fairly large scale, but the concentration on textile tasks of increasing numbers of yeoman families must have slowed down agricultural development.

Population increase and industrialisation are in some ways associated, and a survey of sample parish registers shows that the population of Lancashire almost certainly fell, or at least received a check, in the second half of the seventeenth century. Moreover, there were areas of the county, mainly those concerned with woollen textiles, in which thousands of households were considered too poor to pay hearth tax in 1664; that is to say, their individual cottages were reckoned to be worth less than 20s per annum, or they possessed property worth less than £10. In other words, the slowly growing towns were acquiring many poor people as well as moderately rich fustian dealers or linen drapers. Other very poor areas of Lancashire were the remoter marshlands, like those near the Wyre estuary, and the Furness Fells (although the probate inventories of yeomen in the latter area suggest that much tax evasion was taking place). Lancastrians were prone to wall up their hearths to baulk the 'chimney-man'. But the poverty was real enough, and food supplies were often precarious.

Extraordinarily, this precariousness seems to have been connected with population increases in the early seventeenth century, despite the frequent and terrible outbreaks of bubonic plague. This population upswing was probably related to the plague, in that the latter created vacant homes for would-be married couples, so that the large numbers of plague burials were followed by large numbers of marriages, and then more baptisms. There were new mouths to feed, food became short, and so local near-starvation might follow. The starvation killed rats as well as men, and plague-infected rat fleas, it is supposed, were driven to seek already debilitated human hosts, who then succumbed to the plague. Lancashire and its population centres were stricken in 1557–9, 1586–8 (Manchester, Burnley, Whalley and Clitheroe); 1596–8 (Burnley, the Fylde and Furness); 1622–3 (sometimes held to have been a typhus epidemic); and 1631, when the plague struck savagely at Preston and interrupted markets and trade. These

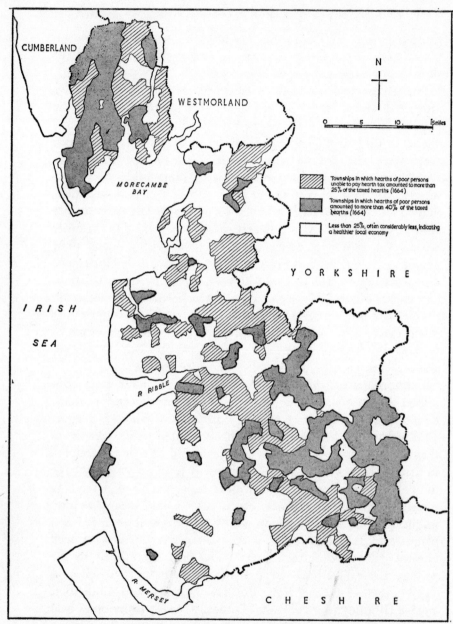

Fig 8   The pattern of poverty in Lancashire, 1664 (from Hearth Tax Lists at the
Public Record Office, E 179/250/11)

visitations ceased after about 1660, but a marked population decline thereafter, in some known parishes, has been associated with later marriages and smaller families. There was some recovery in the early eighteenth century (Figs 9a, 9b).

We now come to the question of Lancashire's total population. Gregory King, who performed the first useful census calculation of England and Wales (1690) counted the number of hearths in Lancashire as 46,961. In the following year, Houghton gave the total hearths as 40,202. If we multiply the mean of these two figures by a commonly used ratio, 4.5, the total population thus obtained, 196,100, may not be far from the mark. Another authority, Gonner, using King's totals, has given a higher figure of 207,090, but certainly the period was one of apparent decline or stagnation of population. This was to be followed by a threefold increase in the eighteenth century.

It is also true that the total number of persons living in Lancashire towns, of any size greater than a village, cannot have exceeded 30,000 in King's time. At the very most, one-sixth to one-seventh of the county population at the end of the Stuart period, were townspeople.

WHAT TO READ

The subject of land use in Tudor Lancashire is dealt with by Professor H. B. Rodgers in *Transactions of the Institute of British Geographers* (1955), and in F. Walker, *Historical Geography of S.W. Lancashire*, Chetham Society, 1939. Dr G. H. Tupling's classic *Economic History of Rossendale* (1927) says much of importance about the hill peasantry of east Lancashire in Tudor and Stuart times. There is a valuable series of articles, based upon an extensive study of Lancashire probate inventories, by Messrs Owen Ashmore and J. J. Bagley, in *The Amateur Historian*, vol 4, nos 4, 5, 6 and 8 (1959–60). There are, in addition, two helpful volumes on sixteenth-century history published by the Chetham Society: Christopher Haigh, *The Last Days of the Lancashire Monasteries* (1969), and Norman Lowe, *The Lancashire Textile Industry in the Sixteenth Century* (1972). A now fully recognised classic carries the story forward: A. P. Wadsworth and Julia de L. Mann, *The Cotton Trade and Industrial Lancashire, 600–1780* (1931), which traces the industry from its deepest roots. Lancashire Puritanism is explored in R. C. Richardson, *Puritanism in North-West England* (1972). In the sphere of population, epidemics and social conditions, there are two important published papers: R. Sharpe France, 'A History of Plague in Lancashire', in the *Historic Society Transactions* for the two counties (vol 90, 1939), and W. G. Howson, 'Plague, Poverty and Population in Parts of North-West England, 1580–1720' in the same *Transactions* (vol 112, 1960). Lancashire nonconformity is discussed in the work of that name by B. Nightingale (1890).

Chapter 4

LANCASHIRE IN THE EIGHTEENTH CENTURY: TOWNS, TRADE AND SOCIETY

THE world's first industrial revolution took place partly in Lancashire in a society, or seed-bed, which helped it to develop in a peculiar way. This 'revolution'—really a change to a town-centred and machine-influenced way of life—did not happen overnight, and the eighteenth century witnessed slow and momentous changes relating to trade, commercial skills, banking and industrial skills all taking effect within the framework of a national or international economy. In the world of Georgian Lancashire, the men who practised these skills could find freedom of action, capital to support their projects, and trading organisations which could help them to sell their goods to growing numbers of people. As population grew, markets widened; and it should be remembered that markets were international also, and that cloth woven on a Lancashire handloom might find its way to the Guinea coast. The fact of home population growth was even more crucial.

THE FACT OF POPULATION GROWTH

It is safe to say that the population of the county increased about threefold between 1690 and 1801 (the date of the first government census), when Lancashire counted 672,700 people, not allowing for the armed forces. This increase, much greater than the less than twofold increase for England and Wales in the same period, seems

D

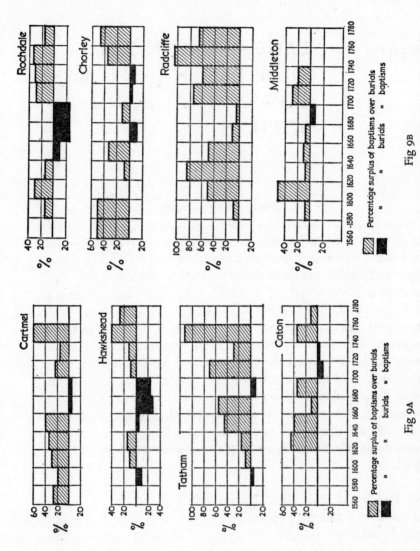

Baptism/burial percentage surpluses (A) north Lancashire country parishes (B) towns and textile districts

to have commenced in earnest after 1730, and hence this flood of people appeared inside seventy years only. Many were incomers from nearby counties, but most were Lancashire-born as far as we can tell, and the upsurge took place in country as well as in town. Hence, the agricultural parish of Croston in central Lancashire roughly doubled in population in this period of seventy years, but in nearby Chorley, there were four people in 1801 where there had been one person a lifetime before. Since it is highly probable that many of the Chorley people were former village dwellers from the same area, the nature of the general increase becomes more apparent.

The immediate influences on this growth were plainly complex. Somewhat lower ages at marriage, extending the child-bearing period for women (resulting in high fertility-rates); more and more young incoming married couples who raised children in the county; the survival of more infants in face of killer diseases like smallpox: greater longevity; all such influences, effective as they may have been, are less certain than the overriding fact that without extensive economic development, this great and growing population could not have been sustained at all. The jobs and food were plainly there.

TOWN AND COUNTRY

So much attention has been directed to the growth of northern industrial towns that it is easy to imagine that the population increases were also town-centred. This was certainly not true of eighteenth-century south Lancashire. Even in 1801, there were only 26 towns in Lancashire with a population of more than 2,000, and of these, only Manchester-Salford and Liverpool had passed the 20,000 mark. These 26 towns, most of them old-established market centres which appear in Fig 6, contained not much more than a third of the Lancashire population, whereas by 1851, two-thirds of the county population lived in towns and cities. Yet, a hundred years before that, towns like Burnley, Bolton and Blackburn had contained fewer than 1,000 families apiece. Bolton, with its two main streets near its market cross, its warehouses and its few hundred yards of housing, was typical of the larger textile towns.

Much of the eighteenth-century population increase, then, was taking place outside Bolton and the other towns, in small hamlets or folds containing weavers, spinners, dyers, bleachers and coal-miners. Hence, if we look at the baptisms and burials in the parish registers of Deane, a district just west of Bolton, which is partly rural and partly suburban even today, we find that the numbers of people baptised and buried in that extensive parish increased between two and three times between the 1740s and the 1790s. This world of hamlets, tiny collieries and weavers' houses can still be seen in the superb ordnance survey map (6in) of 1846, and much of south Lancashire was of such a character. The village of Deane, now part of Bolton, still has some of its rural atmosphere, and was overrun by building only in Victorian times.

In north and west Lancashire, eighteenth-century population growth was somewhat slower, although it was still striking, especially in the period 1740–60, and the country districts sent steady streams of migrants to the towns. The north of England provided the great majority of the workers for the Industrial Revolution, and there was little movement from the southern counties.

MORE FOOD AND MORE JOBS

There were, then, more people in the villages as well as in the towns. How were the greater numbers of people kept alive? It is certain that Lancashire could not support its multitudes from the produce of its fields. The Quaker grocer of Lancaster, William Stout, writing of the year 1729, remarked that 'our market was mostly suplyed with meale out of Westmorland', and 'corn was continually brought into Liverpoole till harvest', some of it from Hamburg. But the potato, that supporter of populations, had already made its appearance in west Lancashire, and by 1727 it was 'plenty and cheap'. Much food was carried into local ports by coastal vessels from other counties, and droves of cattle from Scotland came into Lancashire and the north. But the potato came to play a crucial role, and the manuscript Journal of Richard Latham of Scarisbrick (1699–1767), a west Lancashire yeoman, shows not only that he grew this crop, but that he also grew the carrots and greenstuff which were soon to come in quantity from the Lancashire plain into the great town of Liverpool.

This did not represent an 'agricultural revolution', although there were (as in the above case) a few signs of specialisation in food production. Lancashire was sustained by the growth of trade and the increase of jobs in town and country. Many countrymen managed to do two jobs, smallholding and weaving, and this was especially true of east Lancashire. The parish registers of Newchurch (1705) and Haslingden (1722) show that more than one-third of the persons regularly recorded there were 'weavers'. The largely rural chapelry of Colne, at the end of the century, was to list weavers in hundreds and wool-combers in dozens in its parish registers, especially in Barrowford and Trawden. But country industries were not confined to east Lancashire, and Woodplumpton, in the countryside about four miles north-west of Preston, had its scores of linen weavers, while Walton-le-Dale, on the other side of the Ribble, heard the clack of scores of looms. Such industry was stimulated by an unprecedented growth of trade.

THE GROWTH OF LIVERPOOL AND MANCHESTER

The growth of world and national trade is exemplified in the story of Liverpool. In 1660 it had been a place of a few streets near an old castle: Tithebarn, Dale, Chapel, Water and Castle Streets. As a small agriculturally-based community, it had had a growing trade in salt in the seventeenth century, and had dealt with French and Spanish traders in carrying spices, wines, iron and copper. After the Civil War, a small trade with the West Indies appeared, and in 1707–19, Liverpool Corporation developed the town's first real dock at the Pool. Thereafter Liverpool's success had a solid foundation in the salt exports of Cheshire and the coal of the Prescot area which was used to boil the salt for refining. The import of tobacco and sugar, connected with the 'triangular' Guinea-Atlantic trade of which slaving was a part, gave indirect stimulus to cloth export and hence to Lancashire's rural textile industries. Before 1770 about one-third of the Lancashire cloth export went to the slave coast of west Africa, and about one-half to the West Indian and American colonies. Both cotton goods and woollens were exported, as well as great quantities of linen from west Lancashire handlooms.

Meanwhile, coal supplies came in quantity from the Sankey Canal (opened 1757), road communications were improved and, with the growth of the shipping industry, came the manufacture of iron fittings, ropes and sailcoth (made from Lancashire linen), as well as sugar refining and earthenware. Liverpool became established as the main cotton importer after 1785. The town's population moved from 5,000 (1700) to 25,000 (1760), and then to 77,553 for Liverpool parish (1801). At the beginning of the century it had had some 28 streets, and by 1773 it had about 230. The growth of the other Lancashire port, Lancaster, was more modest, but it, too, shared in the benefits of overseas trade in sugar and tobacco.

Manchester did not grow quite so quickly as Liverpool; it had had more people (about 8,000) in 1700, and rather fewer (70,400) in 1801. Yet it was a centre of commerce, with packhorse routes and roads converging upon it from north and south. In the eighteenth century, its growing merchant class set about the improvement of its road and river communications, and the Mersey & Irwell Navigation was improved in 1736. The Bridgwater Canal (opened in sections from 1761) brought coal into western Manchester from the Worsley mines, and was later connected with the Mersey at Runcorn Gap (1776), thus opening a vital link between the two great commercial centres.

Meanwhile, with the improvement of the roads, the local traders commenced to use waggons instead of packhorses, and the Manchester Man appeared, travelling with cloth patterns in his bag to 'towns all over the kingdom'. Manchester's linen-drapers and merchants were now in effect employing, by 'putting out' raw material to workers, cutters, dyers, bleachers and printers of fabric, and Manchester smallwares (already famous in the seventeenth century) and linen and check manufactures were increasingly organised on a workshop if not a factory system. Extremely hardworking and frugal—John Aikin claimed that in the early eighteenth century there were not 'above three or four carriages kept in the town'—the merchants and their agents controlled an export trade in textiles through London as well as Liverpool. Most of the merchants were also 'manufacturers'. That is to say, they controlled the various processes of domestic cloth making, and accordingly they had many business contacts in the smaller Lancashire towns, who came to Manchester to do business. By the middle of the century, Manchester had a European reputation for the production of velvets, and was already a collecting ground for specialised skill at the loom.

Velvets required a cotton warp as well as a cotton weft thread, and the demand for such material was to play a significant part in the industrial story set out in the next chapter. The town was also to play a part in the rise of factory industry.

THE OTHER TOWNS

John Aikin, writing in the early 1790s, remarked that 'the Bolton manufacturers almost universally repair to Manchester to sell their goods', ie on three days of the week. Manchester's influence was overrunning other, smaller market centres in the county. Bolton itself had remained fairly small but, like the rest of the textile towns, it passed through a great spurt of growth following 1780. Its population had been rather more than 5,000 in 1773, and it was dependent on country weavers for the fustian stored and sold in its warehouses and market, and on Belfast for the supplies of linen thread used in fustian warp. Like the other, secondary textile towns in Lancashire, it was basically a market town. Its most important manufacturers, as in the other towns, had warehouses or offices in Manchester, and with this growth of centralised commerce, the main roads from Manchester to Bury, Bolton, Wigan, Warrington, Oldham, Ashton, Stockport and Wilmslow had all been turnpiked by 1800.

Samuel Crompton undoubtedly arrested Bolton's tendency to be a partial satellite, if such there was. He produced his spinning mule in 1779, at his then home at Hall i'th' Wood north of the town, and made possible the fine spinning that made Bolton workmanship world-famous. But, as a local study of Bolton remarks, 'The migration from country cottages to larger premises in the town was gradual and had begun well before Crompton's time.' However, the town became scattered with muslin workshops using mule-spun yarn, and the nearby countryside had its bleach works using the soft water of the moorland streams, and its patchwork of fields used for 'crofting' or exposing cloth for whitening. There are bleach works on the same main sites even today.

The scenery near Blackburn was in many ways similar. 'The fields around the town are whitened with the materials lying to bleach', wrote Aikin, in the early 1790s. As in the other growing towns, the warehouses and shops were 'intermixed with good houses, the consequences of commercial wealth'. And there was indeed, a close relationship between the putter-out or merchant in the town and the weaver in the countryside. Some of Blackburn's wealthy 'manufacturers' later became mill-owners.

Blackburn received much of its food from Preston, which in turn imported oatmeal from the Fylde and Furness. Preston, the market and social centre of mid-Lancashire, was a 'handsome, well-built town, with broad regular streets and many good houses'— among them being the Earl of Derby's mansion. It was rendered gay by assemblies and other places of amusement suited to the genteel style of the inhabitants. Aikin drew attention to one cotton mill only, although John Horrocks was building those that made his fortune, and the town was 'not characterised by trade'. Preston, during the 1790s, had a good many of the requirements of such a social centre: a theatre, an assembly room, coffee and newsrooms, a book club, a race course and open spaces in which one could promenade. The other towns, even the older centres like Wigan, had few such amenities, although both Preston and Wigan had a public water supply, as had Blackburn. The only Lancashire town which offered a challenge to Preston was the Liverpool of the age of Roscoe (MP, banker and writer) which was experiencing a cultural renaissance of publishing and scholarship (albeit in the 1770s) as well as humanitarian, anti-slaving sentiment in later decades.

What of all the other Lancastrians? Their lives, too, were changing, and many of them were ready to forsake the loom or the farmyard for the towns. But the typical Lancastrian was still a countryman, speaking his strong dialect, observing the age-old festivals, cunning in the ways of textile work and still living basically on oatmeal. But he was often literate and sometimes well-read, and occasionally he might come from a yeoman family which had worked in domestic industry for generations, like the Ashworths and the Peels and the Horrocks family, all mill-builders. His was an open society. By the end of the century, he and men like him were making money from their small mule-workshops or spinning mills, often converted from corn or other mills; and a very few were even setting up as squires and buying estates. A great many more were now specialised artisans or tradesmen in the industrial countryside or the small towns. Banks were now providing credit for industry in the main centres: professional men and merchants founded banks in Manchester (1771) and Liverpool (1760), and moneylending attorneys had long been scattered about the county, acting as loan-brokers and putting out money at interest.

All this was merely the financial mechanism. It is men who make history, and the next half-century was to see changes such as had never happened in the world before. In the next chapter we shall examine some forces that made for change.

FOR READING AND REFERENCE

Wadsworth and Mann's *Cotton Trade* can be supplemented by G. W. Daniels's *The Early English Cotton Industry* (1920), which deals well with eighteenth-century Lancashire developments. On specific towns and regions, C. F. Carter (ed), *Manchester and its Region* (1962), W. Smith (ed), *A Scientific Survey of Merseyside* (1953), and F. E. Hyde, *Liverpool and the Mersey* (1972), contain a wealth of material including essays or sections on the eighteenth century. The *Victoria County History* contains useful sections on all the Lancashire towns, although the items are apt to be inconsequential. Most Lancashire libraries will contain H. W. Clemesha, *Preston in Amounderness* (1912), W. A. Abram, *History of Blackburn* (1877), and W. Bennett, *History of Burnley* (vol 3, 1948, deals with this period). Like the last-mentioned, C. H. Saxelby (ed), *Bolton Survey* (1st ed 1953, revised ed 1970), has the merit of being up-to-date in presentation. F. A. Bruton, *A Short History of Manchester and Salford* (1924) is useful for its details.

For the contemporary view, the student will find J. Aikin, *A Description of the Country from Thirty to Forty Miles Round Manchester* (1795), obtainable in reference libraries and now in facsimile, a mine of fascinating observations. J. Holt, *General View of the Agriculture of Lancaster* (1795), also now available in facsimile form (1969), is equally interesting. G. J. French, *The Life of Samuel Crompton* (1859), contains a vivid account of eighteenth-century Bolton. The Lancashire Parish Register Society has issued a long and valuable series of published parish registers, including volumes for Deane, Walton-le-Dale and Croston. These are to be found in town reference libraries. The Lancashire Record Office at Preston holds the diary of Richard Latham, referred to in the text. J. D. Marshall (ed), *The Autobiography of William Stout* (1967) is a new edition of a remarkable source book. J. R. Harris (ed), *Liverpool and Merseyside* (1969) has most useful essays on money-lending and poverty in west Lancashire. The population material in this chapter was partly supplied by the Cambridge Group for the Study of Population and Social Structure, a body invaluable to local historians.

Chapter 5   LANCASHIRE
INVENTIONS AND THE
HUMAN BEING

As has already been shown, Lancashire life
was becoming more and more inseparable from the textile
industries. Yet the changes of the eighteenth century hardly
seemed to indicate that a new world was to arise in the rather dank
fields and valleys in the south and east of the county.

By 1750, the English cotton industry was mainly concentrated in
Lancashire, although there was a cotton-linen industry in Scotland.
The most commonly produced fabric was fustian, which has a linen
warp and cotton weft; the warp-thread is that which is laid away
from the weaver in the process of cloth-making on the handloom.
As the alternating threads are open and shut to make the 'shed', and
as the shuttle is passed through this space, so the warp-threads are
subjected to extra strain. Accordingly, strong threads are needed,
and so linen was employed in the fustian industry. Meanwhile,
Lancashire inventors sought to make a cotton thread which was
strong enough for the same purpose.

Despite a series of experiments in machine-spinning, not all of
them in Lancashire, the yarn was spun on the domestic spinning-
wheel before 1750, in homes scattered throughout the countryside.
Fustian-weaving was well established in central Lancashire, and
Manchester had an important velvet industry. The rather weak,
lumpy weft thread of the old-style spinner could be used to make
velvet with its 'furred' surface, and almost any diligent person
could spin yarn of that kind. But the weaving of east Lancashire,

59

then engaged in using both woollen and cotton yarn, was becoming more skilled and more varied.

It was in this territory, in the small town of Bury that John Kay, expert technician and reed-maker—the reed is a comb-like device for spacing out the warp-threads—found a way of making the handloom more efficient. Hitherto, the broad type of handloom had been a clumsy object, requiring two men to throw the shuttle from one side to the other. Kay's flying shuttle was a mechanically propelled shuttle on small wheels, 'fired' from one side to the other by 'pickers' (strikers) worked by a lanyard which the weaver held in one hand. Hence one man could work a broad loom on his own at a much greater speed. Although the invention was made in 1733, it was nearly a generation later that it became fully established in central Lancashire cotton-weaving.

Thanks partially to Kay's invention, the shortage of good weft became acute, especially during the Seven Years War (1756–63) and, stimulated by a Royal Society of Arts award scheme, skilful contrivers were at work to solve the problem. In this way James Hargreaves, a former weaver of Standhill near Blackburn, an inventor with more than one achievement to his name, produced the jenny (1764). This was in essence a framework with a hand-cranked device that fed a row of bobbins with yarn, and hence simulated a row of hand-spinners. A carriage imitated the walking to and fro of the spinners, and a lifting wire or bar enabled the machine to impart the twist to each thread as it was fed on to the top of each bobbin.

The first jennies (the word means 'engine') were small; later ones were too large for the room of a cottage, and so this machine tended to be moved into small workshops or even factories, where it remained a hand-operated device. Although it survived the first generation of cotton mills, it also aided the destruction of the fireside spinner, with his or her addition to family earnings. For a time, it greatly increased such earnings and, vastly, the output of weft yarn. By the 1780s, somewhere between 5,000 and 10,000 families in Lancashire were dependent upon it, although the American

War of Independence, with the first factories, had brought a severe crisis.

These inventions, then, affected the lives of thousands, and were to influence the destinies of millions more indirectly. The problem of strong warp yarn, preferably of cotton, remained a serious one, and was solved by the development of the water-frame and the mule. The first of these was early installed in the factory or cotton 'mill', a form of productive organisation even more potent than the inventions themselves. Yet the factory machinery was based on two simple concepts, both directed to the making of strong warp. One of these, the use of frictional rollers to draw out the fibres of cotton before spinning, had already been developed by Lewis Paul in 1738; the other was a long-used spinning device known as the flier, which spun the thread as it was wound on to a bobbin. Richard Arkwright, the Preston-born barber, used other men's ideas to combine these two concepts and to make the water-frame, so called because it could be driven by water power in a factory. The frame produced the strong thread which was needed.

After building mills in Derbyshire, Arkwright erected one at Birkacre near Chorley in 1777. Collinson and Watson started a mill in Preston in the same year, and Robert Peel, of the famous family, had opened a mill at Bury in 1774. Small mills were at first common, many of them converted from other uses.

The domestic worker, scattered through the Lancashire folds and lanes, was feeling the pressure of workshop- and factory-produced yarn during the years of the American War of Independence, and the stoppage of cotton supplies from America in 1779, resulting in unemployment and misery, brought bitter feelings into the open. Rioters in central Lancashire attacked Arkwright's factory at Birkacre, but they also directed their anger at jenny workshops at Aspull, Leigh, Golborne, Bolton, Blackburn and Balderstone. It is interesting to note that jennies below twenty-four spindles in capacity were spared; the attackers were protesting at the stealing of work by the larger machines and by the richer employers who owned them. Thus began an age of industrial tension and conflict, in which domestic workers took a leading part. It is quite untrue that factories were seats of class warfare at this stage, but they were a part-cause of it.

Meanwhile, the factory system grew apace, but not before yet another inventor had profoundly influenced local events. Very few of Lancashire's textile inventors were armchair men, and the need for strong but fine warp yarn, still in short supply, brought Samuel Crompton of Bolton, another southern Lancastrian with years of textile experience, into the field with his spinning mule (1779). This combined the form and operation of the jenny with Arkwright-type rollers, and the device is easily recognised by the moving wheeled carriage. Its impact was so great that Bolton became the centre of fine cotton spinning, and its operators could extract fantastic lengths of thread from a pound of cotton. In the meantime it remained a hand-powered machine, used in small workshops in Bolton yards and spinning the fine yarn used in muslin weaving. (Only in early 1973 were the last Lancashire mules removed from a factory in Farnworth, after the machine, power-driven in huge mills, had made the international reputation of the Bolton area.)

But there was no sudden transition from the small workshop to the large factory; small mills were common, and the relatively few large mills, which tended to stand in detached situations, were financed by the merchant capital of the great dealers in fustian and calico like Peter Drinkwater and Joseph Thackeray at Manchester, or William Douglas and the Peels, each of whom had a mill in the southern or Manchester area. By 1800 there was a visible concentration of mills in the latter district, but there were many 'country' mills also.

THE SIGNIFICANCE OF THE FACTORY

The factory or mill has rightly been seen as representing a totally new way of industrial life, with its insistence on rules and discipline, and its strict time-keeping, together with the dictation of work speeds enforced by powered machinery. The elegant little belfries of the old mills represented a strait-jacket on a generation which had kept its own inner time and worked by the sun and the seasons. However, the adult male factory hand was in a clear minority, sometimes whole families were recruited in order to provide supplies of child or female labour, as in the case of the Peels at Bury. Many mill-owners used 'apprentice' children from distant poor law authorities, and the treatment of these unfortunates varied according to situation and motive on the part of owner or overlooker. There has been some controversy over the general treatment of mill children; the implied or direct condemnations by Sir Robert Peel the elder, or Robert Owen, make much of it otiose.

The factories' effect on the home and the family was for the time being more momentous. Carding and spinning had been transferred to the factory almost completely by the 1790s, and the women and children who would have worked at those jobs applied themselves to the loom instead. The cotton weaver, whose machine remained hand-operated, multiplied in thousands, whether making muslins or coarser fabrics like calico, and cotton weaving began to creep into the former woollen and worsted areas like Rossendale, calico taking over in Colne.

THE WEAVERS

The weaver enjoyed a nominal freedom that the factory worker did not, but the raw material was not his, he was often dependent upon a master for warps and wages, and he was tied to an exhausting and often unhealthy job. There were, however, many different types of weaver, and much of the work was done in rural conditions. Town weavers in Bolton and Blackburn often occupied cellars, and among these would be the weavers of fancy goods, the skilled men whose work earned them high wages in the 1790s. The trade was booming until the end of that decade, and migrants flooded into the towns from the abandoned lead mines of Derbyshire, from unemployed woollen looms in east Lancashire, from sailcloth looms in Warrington, or the fields and farms of the north west. It was stated that if a woman's husband (in eg Wigan) enlisted in the Napoleonic Wars, and she then turned weaver and instructed her children in the art, then the family might '[live] better since [the] husband enlisted than before' (1799). But the trade was exposed to the most violent fluctuations, and the steady growth of the weaving element through the whole of south and east Lancashire compounded a vulnerable population.

By 1830, the weavers in Lancashire alone had reached an estimated 100,000, and most of these were in Bolton and Preston districts, and in the eastern towns and valleys. Many of these must have been part-timers working in the countryside. Between one in six and one in seven of the population of Lancashire seems to have been dependent upon handloom weaving at the peak of the industry, although it should be borne in mind that many families had between two and three looms. These people were to be exposed to grim privation in the generation following the Napoleonic Wars. Another major invention, that of powerloom weaving, was to have vast repercussions, in that the handloom weaver was to be threatened by factory machinery and was to be inexorably destroyed as a member of an occupational group.

FACTORY WORKERS AND MASTERS

What of the factory workers? Although the statistics of the age are unreliable, we know that the Manchester 'area' (including, presumably, Bolton and Bury) contained at the end of the wars between 43 and 70 cotton mills with an average of just over 300 persons to a mill (1815–16). The total labour force, then, cannot have exceeded 23,000 people, chiefly women and children. Since the population of the same area, Salford Hundred, was then about 400,000, the factory worker was as yet hardly typical.

The employing class of mill-owners was made up of a varied and remarkable group of men, many of whom had arisen not from the poorest circumstances, but from other branches of the textile industry, like merchanting and putting-out. Some, like the Eccles family of Darwen and Blackburn, or the Sudells of the latter town, or the already mentioned and famous Peels, were of yeoman origin, and each of these families had risen far by the early 1800s. Some employers started their careers as grocers or drapers, and a good many commenced with little education. Climbing the social ladder (social mobility) there often was, but it could be spread over two or three generations.

Even in 1831, Lancashire owed a great deal of its individually accumulated wealth to commerce rather than to factory production. In that year, Liverpool had more 'capitalists, bankers, professional and other educated men' in its immediate area than any place in Lancashire, and more than twice as many *pro rata* as Manchester. Nevertheless, a solid group of industrialists was appearing in the latter place, and there were 186 spinning-mill owners in Manchester in 1824, and 354 silk and cotton 'manufacturers'. These were accompanied by a mass of small masters in the textile finishing trades, or in putting-out, and by an almost equally numerous group of rich merchants. It is not surprising that the new owning class did not make itself felt politically and administratively until the 1840s. After 1835, more industrialists became magistrates; until then the smell of industry had been a positive disqualification for many.

SOME FURTHER READING

There are many books on the Lancashire textile industry of this age. The studies by Wadsworth and Mann, and by G. W. Daniels, referred to at the end of the previous chapter, are of paramount importance, but the reader who is prepared to get his head down will derive enormous pleasure from the classic by Paul Mantoux, *The Industrial Revolution in the Eighteenth Century* (1928, reprinted many times), which gives essential background. On the results of recent research into technology and industrial archaeology, see C. Aspin and S. D. Chapman, *James Hargreaves and the Spinning Jenny* (1964), O. Ashmore, *The Industrial Archaeology of Lancashire* (1969), and, for more complex details, R. L. Hills, *Power in the Industrial Revolution* (1970). But the student will learn even more by visiting the Higher Mill Museum at Helmshore, or the Lewis Textile Museum at Blackburn, or the North Western Museum of Science and Industry, Manchester.

On the more human side, F. Collier, *The Family Economy of the Working Classes, 1784–1833* (1964), and Unwin, Hulme and Taylor, *Samuel Oldknow and the Arkwrights* (2nd ed 1968), or French's *Life of Crompton*, already cited, are revealing. D. Bythell, *The Handloom Weavers* (1969), provides thorough documentation, and E. P. Thompson, *The Making of the English Working Class* (1963), adds a humane dimension.

Chapter 6   THE NEW TOWNS,
1790–1830

BEFORE 1830, Lancashire had only two great towns, Manchester and Liverpool. The rest of the south and east of the county consisted of a mass of growing industrial communities surrounded by countryside. As the agricultural writer John Holt put it, cottages were built 'near large factories, being frequently built in long ranges adjoining together' (1795). Consequently the development of these communities was a piecemeal affair, resulting in strings of settlements along the valley bottoms of Rossendale or those of the country north of Rochdale. In the areas nearer Manchester, stone cottages gave way to those of the warm, hand-made brick that can sometimes still be seen on the outskirts of Bolton or Stockport. The latter type often housed miners as well as textile workers, for the tiny lane-side collieries nourished many a small settlement in a remote corner. For many people who know east Lancashire well, this enclosed world, marked by a factory chimney at the foot of a moor or in the bottom of a ravine, is typical of the region.

THE NATURE OF TOWN GROWTH
Why, then, were so many appalling social and sanitary ills associated with the growth of industrialism? Most of the new industrial towns remained physically quite small until well after Victoria's accession in 1837, and the point to remember about them is that they grew *intensively* rather than extensively, concentrating their building in existing yards and alleys or on small plots and orchards. This cramming in of people was partly the result of opportunism

66

stimulated by rocketing land values, and partly that of absence of controls over a rapacity which was by no means confined to a few major landowners. Few of the speculators can have really understood or cared about the evils that might follow.

Unfortunately, the early census figures are not sub-divided accurately into small enough districts to give us a clear idea of the degree of the worst overcrowding in localities, although a study of the town maps of the time can be revealing. Baines's map of Bolton (1824) shows that a very high proportion of the population of that town was contained in less than half a square mile, and was concentrated behind both frontages of the main thoroughfare of Deansgate. The joint townships of Great and Little Bolton grew by nearly 24,000 people between 1801 and 1831, and much of the influx of migrants came into this small area, just as the large numbers who were born in the town made their homes within it.

A few of the darker alleyways in this crowded area remained for inspection until a few years ago. One of them, known as Velvet Walks, consisted of three-storey houses overlooking a narrow yard down which ran the 'slops' in a central gutter. The houses, when demolished about 1961, proved to be reasonably well built (the writer took some building technologists to look at them), and it is clear that the real social problems of the time were less concerned with dampness and coldness than with accumulation of filth, airlessness and overcrowding. Whole families occupied one room, and Bolton soon had thousands of cellar dwellings.

How far was this typical of Lancashire towns in general? Preston shared many of Bolton's problems, in that intensive building and overcrowding took place behind the main thoroughfares. Yet, only a short distance from these squalid areas were open spaces, walks and roomy squares. Burnley, in the words of the town's historian, Mr Walter Bennett, was rapidly acquiring 'back-to-back houses, cellar dwellings, tenement houses, grouped together to form dismal streets or arranged round a narrow court to form a compact group', especially at places like Hill Top, Wapping and Thorneybank. Such names, quite common in these towns, told in bizarre fashion of the country spots which were being invaded. In

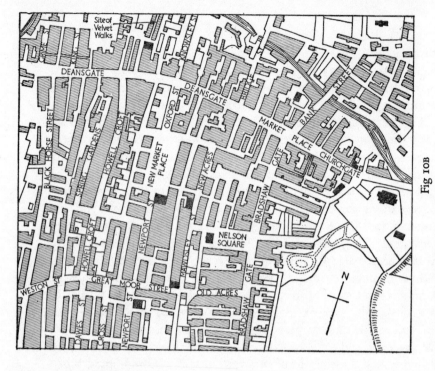

Fig 10B

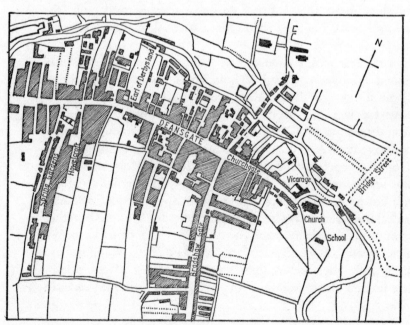

Fig 10A

Central area of Bolton (A) in 1793, (B) in 1824 (detail from Baines's map of 1824)

Wigan, the All Saints Ward, in the vicinity of the parish church, was also seriously congested. But in Wigan, as around the other towns, there was much open-type development along the main roads, and hence the most terrible health hazards did not affect all dwellers equally. Indeed, it is probable that a majority of Lancashire workpeople remained within sight and sound of the country, a probability which accounts for the survival of most of them in face of the most hideous lack of sanitation.

In a great town like Manchester, large, regular blocks of working-class habitations developed early in a district like New Cross, laid out between the Oldham Road and the Rochdale Canal. This layout dated at least from the time of Laurent's map of Manchester, surveyed in the 1790s, and in much less than a generation New Cross had become a great working-class concentration, strongly inclined to Luddism or extreme radicalism, just as it was later associated with Chartism. It just as rapidly became, during the bitter years after the Napoleonic Wars, a near-slum. It is now almost wholly demolished. Manchester, in any case, was not representative of Lancashire, and few of the other towns had great undifferentiated areas of this kind.

A mixture of poverty, low rents, the relative cost of land in town centres, rapacity uncontrolled by local government and an inability to get accommodation elsewhere, allied, perhaps, to the typical countryman's imperviousness to muck and its odour; each of these factors added into a whole helps to explain the conditions in which more and more immigrants found themselves living. It is untrue that people 'flooded' into these towns; an immigrant flow of three families a week for a generation would have accounted for the total increase of the Bolton population between 1801 and 1831. But the result, an industrial town, was nevertheless new in kind, creating at once new types of social awareness and almost insuperable living problems.

LOCAL NON-GOVERNMENT

The Lancashire towns of the nineteenth century expanded with unprecedented rapidity in an age which apparently did not know how to make a properly designed sewer (until the 1850s), and which had insufficient control over property to insist upon adequate drainage. The supply of water was a different matter; Preston had had a water supply of sorts in the eighteenth century, and Bolton received water from its fine Belmont reservoir as early as 1824, through a private company. Water could be sold on a commercial basis, but drains, especially when one could always blame one's neighbour for not laying them, appeared to carry no profit.

Yet there were stirrings of administrative response. Burnley had Improvement Commissioners as early as 1819, although the members of this worthy body—property owners who replaced the democratic church vestry—saw their functions very narrowly, and were more disturbed by drunkenness than filth. Bolton's Trustees, two separate bodies for the 'Great' and 'Little' parts of the town, could cause the water from a spring to be directed into a public trough, or order the removal of dung from a footway. Even when the town received its modern-type local government, in the form of an elected town council following 1837, there was little transformation. Most towns came to be governed by a mixture of bodies: the local church vestries (the most ancient form of local government), Courts Leet (another ancient institution), Commissioners of Sewers, Highway Committees and, in the years following 1834, Poor Law Guardians.

The real business of public improvement took more than half a century to put under way, and this appalling fact is sometimes reflected in the time-lag in the appointment of suitable institutions. Hence, Blackburn had Police Commissioners in 1803, but no Improvement Commissioners until 1847. Haslingden, typical of an industrial district outside the main towns, had no Local Board of Health until 1875, and in a place like this, as late as 1871, one might find a 'building used by some two hundred persons as a joint privy'.

To blame the absence of suitable governmental institutions for what took place is to use a misleading argument. The basic problem was a lack of town leadership which both understood and cared about these matters; private business, which produced both mills and houses, was sacrosanct and powerful, and as some scattered experiments showed, it had the power to make improvements for those who laboured. It neither used that power, nor, on a larger scale, did it patronise the technological skill which could have made that power more effective. The England of the manufacturers could direct steam and water with massive effect; but it could not move filth through a pipe without delaying wretchedly for a generation.

THE NEW POPULATIONS

The new generation of town-dwellers found not only filth, but a sense of community which we sometimes call 'class'. People recognised others in the same plight as themselves, or (in the case of the rising middle class) as holding the same type of stake in society. The new working class worked in innumerable scattered establishments, and at first it was certainly not radical in politics. The workman or labourer of the 1790s was likely to be a Church-and-King man, and a Lancashire cotton trade union of that time (combination) declared that 'rioting, or any illegal behaviour, we detest, and are firmly attached to our King and Country'. But this attitude was often replaced by a much more radical one in the following twenty years. Although this subject is explored at greater length in the next chapter, it is relevant here to ask why the new radicalism appeared.

One reason is fairly certain. The town-dwellers felt themselves to be hostages to fortune, with nobody to take responsibility for their welfare. The old gentry of the countryside, and the old order, had taken a nominal responsibility for 'their' labourers, and some country factory owners displayed a similar attitude. The uprooted immigrants were thrown together in large numbers, and they could see more goods and more wealth than they had ever seen before. Possessors of property feared this mass of people, uncontrolled by our modern police forces and capable of rioting in times of privation. The working-class townspeople were herded anonymously together, and developed common social and institutional interests also: friendly societies, illegal trade unions and religious groups. The working man learned that he had to cater for his own interests; often nobody else would.

The dissenting, nonconformist breakaway from the grip of the established church, which in turn reflects this social and class division of town society, is well displayed in the Lancashire towns. By 1824, 5 important Lancashire towns outside Manchester (Blackburn, Burnley, Bury, Wigan and Warrington) had between them 8 Anglican churches, 6 Roman Catholic churches and no fewer than 30 dissenting chapels. The latter had almost all appeared after 1790. They represented both middle- and working-class groups, and the most influential type of nonconformity, Methodism, was both the strongest and the least radical. In Manchester, the Catholics were very strong by 1824, helped by the growing Irish influx. The majority of town workers—and this must be very strongly stressed indeed—remained untouched by religion, and even Methodism reached out to a distinct minority. The other groups—Independents, Baptists and Unitarians, as well as Quakers —were comparably small.

The chapels and churches provided Sunday Schools, and probably saved the new population from sinking further into illiteracy. Recent research has indicated very strongly that literacy declined under industrialism at this stage, and the masses of children in the newer towns were not catered for by adequate schools, which were in turn greatly outnumbered by other types of establishment, inns and taverns. Just as the chapels suggest the new outlooks which town life encouraged, so the drinking places indicate the working man's escape from its barrenness.

Generally, the newly arisen towns were cheerless places, not always because they lacked fine houses or public buildings—there was a wave of prestige building in the years 1819–24—but because of the hours and conditions to which working people were becoming accustomed. As the journalist P. A. Whittle said of the inhabitants of Blackburn: 'Hard work is the rule of their life.' Women and children frequently worked a sixty- or even a seventy-hour week, but male handloom weavers enjoyed 'play days' through lack of work. The old domestic workers' holidays and fair days were being expunged by factory owners in the 1830s. The beerhouse, greatly increased in numbers by the Beer Act of 1830 designed to encourage beer consumption as an 'antidote' to spirit drinking, offered a brief but smoky refuge. Home life, too, suffered from the lack of domestic training on the part of the thousands of factory women and girls, and child mortality rose. Soot fell on washing unchecked, and filth reeked in the back yard and alley; there was little to encourage cleanliness and domestic pride. Sports and pastimes, especially in the mining districts, tended to be brutal, like the shin-kicking game known as 'purring'.

Nevertheless, the growing Lancashire towns showed a remarkable variety that is often overlooked. Groups of houses stood amid gardens and even trees, and the affluent lived almost side by side with the poor. Small colonies of dwellings with their workplaces lay around the edges of the built-up areas. This meant that some groups of the industrial workers and their families did in fact enjoy fresh air and spring water, just as the mill-owners, lawyers and professional people generally were often exposed to cholera or typhoid.

This was the position about 1830. Although many mill-owners and employers still lived near their factories and workplaces, a slow separation out was beginning, especially in a great town like Manchester, where middle-class citizens were moving to villas in Cheetham Hill and Broughton, and later to Rusholme. Eventually, in the mid-century, most of the cotton towns had growing or incipient middle-class suburbs, usually to the west of the towns themselves, and their most affluent industrialists and leaders were going even farther afield. It is possible that these developments, which made it feasible for the moneyed groups to escape (and in a very real sense abdicate) their responsibilities, delayed full sanitary reform for at least half a generation. But we cannot be sure about this, for the problem of muck appeared insuperable for decades of this period, and certainly looked so in 1830.

FURTHER READING

Although the volumes recommended in the notes to Chapter 4 will be found useful, we also recommend to the reader an especially fascinating exercise, that he looks through the descriptions of towns in Edward Baines's *History, Directory and Gazetteer of the County Palatine of Lancaster* (2 vols, 1824)—a remarkable work available in almost any good Lancashire reference library, and now available in a new edition (1968). The separate volume of *Illustrations* to the above work was republished in facsimile by E. J. Morten (1969), and is invaluable. The reader might then go on to look at Baines's great county history (1836) mentioned in Chapter 1, with its descriptions of the same towns a decade or so later, and its fine illustrations.

Chapter 7   THE WORKER AND HIS
DEFENCES, 1790-1850

THE EARLY UNIONS

THE new town workers, as we have seen, did not consist of an undifferentiated mass of people, in which each man was like the next. The majority of people worked at home or in small workshops pursuing a variety of trades, of which handloom weaving was the most important. Cotton-factory workers, many of whom were children, were in the minority for much of the period 1790-1850, and a substantial number of these did not work in towns as such. There is much evidence, nevertheless, that many industrial workers began to feel a sharp sense of group identity, a feeling of belonging to a subordinate, ill-used section in society. At first, this sense of belonging must have applied to one's own trade group only, and widespread association was hindered (although not stopped) by the repressive Combination Acts of 1799-1824.

These Acts were of course aimed at trades unionism, and unions of every kind were treated as criminal conspiracies by a government which had been terrified by the French Revolution. Pitt's government tried just as vigorously to put down political radicalism, which in Manchester in the early 1790s was led by the merchant Thomas Walker, and which was expressed through the *Manchester Herald* newspaper (1792-3). Although Walker had working men among his supporters, the typical weaver or labourer was then, as already mentioned, probably a Church-and-King man, and much working-class activity of the period was *economic*. Spinners' trade unions from several Lancashire towns tried to form a federation in 1792, miners began to combine also, and such loose organisations were never far from violence. Lancashire had a long tradition of opposition to employment-reducing inventions (angry rioters had destroyed carding and spinning machines in the Bolton and Wigan districts in 1779), and Luddite risings were to spread in the cotton districts in 1812, especially in Stockport, Oldham, Macclesfield, Middleton and in the Bolton area.

However, innumerable people also clubbed together in a much more constructive spirit to form friendly societies, which by 1812 were to be found in hundreds in south and east Lancashire. These paid out small sickness benefits and other payments, and were the worker's chief form of social security.

WORKING-CLASS RADICALISM

Some of these bodies were unquestionably disguised trade clubs or unions. Although such organisations played some part in defending the workman, he turned increasingly to *political* solutions through radicalism, and in 1819, the Hampden clubs (numerous in south Lancashire) and the radical societies, sent contingents to the Peterloo demonstration by the score. It was in these years that weavers and other domestic workers were debating complete suffrage—a downright revolutionary consideration in face of an aristocratic government and a severely limited franchise—and points which went to make up the (later) People's Charter, like annual parliaments, equal electoral districts and payment of members of parliament. The growing towns of Lancashire, meanwhile, had little parliamentary representation; the little old town of Clitheroe returned an MP, as did Newton-le-Willows, while Blackburn or Oldham had no MP at all, and Manchester likewise lacked a single member. The 1832 Reform Act changed this situation.

How powerful were these radical movements? When Henry Hunt, the 'Orator' of Peterloo, became a parliamentary candidate for Preston in 1820, he received 1,127 votes out of a total electorate of 6,000 or so, in a town in which virtually all adult males had the vote (through an accident of history), and which had many weavers and similar workers. But in December 1830, he at last achieved a majority in a straight fight, at a time of intense reform agitation, winning 3,730 votes against E. G. Stanley's 3,392. It should be remembered that voting was open and public and that corruption was often brought to bear. However, the indication here is that perhaps half of the new industrial masses could think in radical terms. Sheer privation and insecurity was to broaden this movement in a number of fields.

At worst, this movement could return to the tactics of desperate machine-breaking, as in east Lancashire in 1826, when a fairly widespread introduction of power-looms provoked bitter reprisals from handloom weavers already suffering under the recession of 1825-6.

MECHANICS AND CO-OPERATORS

But there was, as always, a more constructive side to working-class organisation. There had long been an urge to literacy on the part of skilled workers—John Holt, writing in 1795, had commented of Lancashire that 'There are more readers amongst the lower class of people, it is supposed, than in any part of the kingdom.' Although the rapid growth of the towns caused many children to go without the barest schooling, the artisan passion for education did not diminish, and the mechanics' institute movement surged forward in 1824-5, with the formation of these voluntary centres of learning in Manchester, Liverpool, Warrington, Wigan, Bolton, Ashton-under-Lyne and numerous smaller places in the county. Hampden Clubs and Political (radical) Unions went to great pains to build up 'reading societies' and permanent newsrooms and reading-rooms; highly necessary when stamp, advertisement and paper duties on newspapers sent up the price of a copy to the value of several hours' wage-equivalent. Cobbett's *Political Register* was also widely read and an unstamped (illegal) press circulated among the rebels. Chapel communities, strong in all the industrial towns, provided a literate and sometimes politically conscious public, although Wesleyan Methodists could be passionately anti-radical.

Friendly societies, meanwhile, became organised on a regional and then a national basis, which meant that the insecure local societies could now be safeguarded by professional advice and powerful finances. The Manchester Unity of Oddfellows developed out of local societies in Manchester in 1810–16, and by 1832, the Unity claimed to have 561 lodges and 31,000 members, most of them in the north-west. The other Oddfellows' orders, the Grand United and the National Independent, like the Foresters and the Ancient Shepherds, all came to be strong in the north.

However, these bodies were divorced from politics, and the effective Lancashire working-class movement was one of successive or simultaneous campaigns and interests often led by the same people. The main background influence, sometimes a disastrous one, came from Robert Owen, who saw co-operative communities as providing an alternative to the unbridled and often destructive individualism of crude free enterprise. Numerous Owenite co-operative societies were formed in south Lancashire in 1829–32, most of them for the retailing of groceries, although two of the most prominent local leaders, Elijah Dixon and E. T. Craig, took part in 'communitarian' experiments—Dixon in one on Chat Moss! Each was a mechanics' institute member and Peterloo veteran. The ultimate aim of many of these Owenite societies was that of going on to *productive* co-operation and then later including an agricultural sector to make a complete community. The Rochdale Pioneers of 1844, who included several Owenites, settled mainly for retail distribution of good food with the all-important dividend, and they were vastly successful by contrast. Some would argue that the movement lost its soul nevertheless.

FACTORY REFORM

Yet another Owenite, the cotton spinner, Catholic and radical of Manchester, John Doherty, followed his master's precepts in attempting to organise not only the cotton spinners (1829), but a general union of all trades, The National Union for the Protection of Labour (1830), which rapidly expanded for a few years. Doherty, a remarkable man, was interested in factory reform, and as Owen's impractical schemes for a moral take-over of society collapsed, the much more widely based factory movement went from strength to strength, unifying local trade unionists, doctors and ministers. This movement had stirred occasionally in the 1820s, demanding an 11-hour day for children under sixteen instead of the 12 hours permitted by the Factory Act of 1819.

In 1831 the Yorkshire land agent Richard Oastler was leading the historic campaign for the 10-hour day, supported by Doherty and his trade union colleagues. The latter organised Ten Hours Committees through Lancashire and Cheshire, and both radicals and some Tories gave backing to the movement, which was hotly opposed by the *Manchester Guardian* and the factory owners, who saw it as gross interference with the liberty of the employer. Owen's own interference with the same movement—he rushed ahead of it by demanding an 8-hour day, and his national trade union movement, supposed to enforce the new order, collapsed in 1834—provided a temporary setback. The Ten Hours Committees re-emerged in the forties, however, and this time spread to small towns like Horwich and Tyldesley or even to factory colonies like those at Farington and Samlesbury. The movement was split into factions, in this case supporters of Oastler and J. R. Stephens on the one hand, and supporters of Lord Ashley (Shaftesbury) on the other. But it was ultimately successful, although the Act of 1847, bringing in the 10 hours' limitation in textile factories, was evaded by many employers, including the Ashworths and Brights. Such employers sought to destroy the Act by using children and young persons on the *relay system*, ie by working them for broken periods of less than 10 hours apiece, but otherwise for as long as they chose. The clear limitation of 10 hours daily was not secured until 1874.

THE NEW POOR LAW AND CHARTISM

The Poor Law Amendment Act of 1834, which sought to establish the notorious union workhouses of the 'Oliver Twist' type, met with much passive resistance in Lancashire (on the part of employers, who feared that their supplies of reserve labour might be driven away) and also with passionate condemnation on the part of working-class radicals. In the depression period of the late thirties, this deep feeling was unquestionably behind the first waves of agitation for the People's Charter. The principles of the latter, based on that of a vote for every adult male, were, as we have seen, well known in Lancashire.

Between March and December 1837, meetings in Manchester made reference to the complete (male) suffrage principle of the Charter, and two suffrage associations appeared in the town in the following year. In September 1838 a vast Chartist meeting on Kersal Moor drew together an estimated 30,000 people, and in this a variety of trades and craft unions took part. A further wave of vitality led to demonstrations in the summer of 1839, when the movement was clearly supported in towns and villages throughout the county. Yet the strength of the support varied greatly from place to place; it was very marked in centres still containing handloom weavers and other domestic workers, like Bolton and Blackburn, and it had many outposts in east and south-east Lancashire, but had little obvious strength in a newer town like St Helens or a commercial centre like Liverpool.

When the Chartist movement rose to its peak of success, in the grim period of 1841–2, when burial rates in all the main Lancashire towns rocketed, branches of the National Charter Association were established even in quite small mill communities like Mossley and Shaw. In August 1842, any differences between physical and moral force Chartists were submerged in the Plug Riots, when demonstrators and rioters in the south-east of the county, and especially at Ashton and Stalybridge, sought to draw out the boiler plugs of the mills to immobilise them. The mills were already on short time. This turn-out was utilised as a means of demonstration for the Charter, and subsequently Feargus O'Connor and fifty-eight other persons were tried for their part in fomenting unrest.

In the following few years, Lancashire radicals and reformers turned to other activities, like the formation of Short Time or Ten Hours Committees, or the promotion of co-operation or trade unionism. Owenite idealism had by no means died, and in the middle years of the century, Lancashire working men, deeply influenced by Owen's and O'Connor's attempts to form self-supporting communities on the land, were still trying to create the occasional centre of co-operative production. Chartism itself surged forth once more in 1847–8, and there were some violent interludes in the towns, but the 'new' co-operators of Rochdale, and the Ten Hour Movement, achieved far more in the way of tangible success. Yet it is unwise to be patronising about the Chartists, whose most radical leader, Ernest Jones, died greatly respected in Manchester some twenty years later. His fellows had pointed the way forward to modern political democracy, however desperately.

SOME READING

There are few works which give even a straightforward introduction to the topics in this chapter, but one can recommend Donald Read, *Peterloo, the Massacre and Its Background* (1958); G. D. H. Cole, *A Century of Co-operation* (1945); and J. T. Ward, *The Factory Movement, 1830–55* (1962). Hovell, *The Chartist Movement* (1925), provides some general background to its subject, and Donald Read's 'Chartism in Manchester' in A. Briggs (ed), *Chartist Studies* (1960), is one of the few original pieces on Lancashire developments in Chartism. There are numerous specialised essays in *Transactions of the Lancashire and Cheshire Antiquarian Society*: Boyson on the Poor Law (1960), Rose on the Plug Plots (1958) and Ward on J. R. Stephens (1958). Hutchins and Harrison, *A History of Factory Legislation* (1926), is still an invaluable work.

Some real evidence, however, is in the pages of Lancashire newspapers of this period, to be found in the relevant public libraries: in eg the *Manchester and Salford Advertiser*, the *Bolton Chronicle* or the *Preston Chronicle*.

Chapter 8   MIDDLE-CLASS
LANCASHIRE

IN the years before the Reform Act of 1832, sections of the Lancashire industrial middle class began to acquire a political as well as a social identity. The non-representation of the new industrial towns in parliament was seen to be a scandal, and the movement for reform was by no means purely radical or restricted to party—H. H. Birley, who led the charge against the Peterloo demonstrators, was one of those who demanded a seat for Manchester, and the great Liverpudlian and Canningite Tory, William Huskisson, was an architect of Free Trade. The sentiments of the latter movement, which demanded an end to undue excise restrictions on international trade, tended to affect businessmen in Victorian Lancashire irrespective of party grouping, but Free Trade did give a powerful impetus to radical movements, including those against the corn laws following 1815. Obviously, such movements could not prosper unless there were Lancashire industrialists in parliament.

A small but strongly radical group in Manchester, with some roots in the pro-Jacobin struggle of the 1790s, and with leanings towards Adam Smith's economics, Benthamite government, Unitarianism, popular education and parliamentary reform, conducted a local campaign against vested interests in parish pump affairs and, through Archibald Prentice, Absolom Watkin, the Potter Brothers and the *Manchester Guardian* (1821), provided a direct link with the Anti-Corn Law League following 1838. These agitators, fewer in number than is often imagined, afford an example of what is called 'middle-class consciousness'. The

82

oppressive corn laws, controlling the inflow of grain from other countries, were designed to keep up the price of corn to benefit the great landowners. The new industrialist groups in Lancashire and elsewhere saw themselves as the real organisers of national wealth and production, and were coming to despise the landed rulers of society who took their right to govern for granted. Meanwhile, as we have seen, *working-class* radicalism adopted a sharp form in the years after 1815, and the middle class tended to see social and political demarcation lines in consequence. The middle class had more to lose.

AFTER REFORM

The 1832 Reform Act gave two seats each to Manchester, Bolton, Blackburn and Oldham, and one each to Ashton, Bury, Rochdale, Salford and Warrington. Wigan, Lancaster, Preston and Liverpool remained as before, Newton (a rotten borough) was disfranchised, and Clitheroe kept its one member.

Voting was restricted to male £10 householders, tenants or owners, so that a town with high rents, like Manchester, benefited; but a poorer town, like Wigan, suffered, with only one in twelve adult males eligible for the vote. Preston, which had had a full male suffrage, had its voters rapidly cut by half. About one-seventh of the adult male population of the Lancashire towns now had the vote, and the anger or frustration of radicals and (later) Chartists is easy to understand. Parliament remained filled with gentry, with some bankers and merchants. A very few radicals now sat for the north-west; Joseph Brotherton (Salford) spoke for the Manchester men, and Fielden and Cobbett were elected for Oldham (1832).

SOCIAL EXCLUSION

At the time of the Reform Act, Lancashire landed society still monopolised the control of county affairs through the magistracy, or commission of the peace. Since most of the gentry lived in the north of the county, there was a severe shortage of magistrates in the industrial south. In Lonsdale Hundred, there was one magistrate to 1,926 persons, but in industrial Salford Hundred (which included Bolton and Manchester) there was one to 14,663 (1821).

The selection of magistrates, controlled by leading county figures like Bootle Wilbraham (of Lathom, later Lord Skelmersdale) and Lord Derby, was limited to 'Gentlemen of independent property with suitable character and abilities'—in practice, those who were of old lineage, Anglican and conventionally educated. However, as more and more cotton manufacturers bought estates and set up as minor gentry, the pressures to admit them to the bench became greater, and as the social problems of south Lancashire multiplied, especially in the turbulent forties, the imbalance was partly corrected. Indeed, the bar against manufacturers was effectively overcome by 1841, and 257 new magisterial appointments were made in 1842–51, many of them from industry, although the bench was still half-composed of landed gentry in that decade.

The political significance of this galling exclusion should not be overlooked; the manufacturers of south Lancashire had additional reason for disliking the older gentry before the forties.

THE RADICAL ATTACK

The new, thrusting radical Manchester group, to which allusion has been made, united against the Tory holders of office in their own town to fight the Police Commission and the Court Leet. Led by Richard Cobden, they brought about the incorporation of Manchester in 1838 in the face of the older vested interests. In Bolton, likewise, Henry Ashworth and C. J. Derbyshire led a simultaneous battle for incorporation (1838), bringing about an important anti-Tory, non-conformist and radical triumph. In so doing, these forces were trying to correct middle-class lack of experience in local or administrative office.

However, their struggle is, again, a matter of political significance. The sanitary problems of the towns were, for the time being, outside the sphere of effective interest of large sections of the middle class, and there was also a middle-class movement from the industrial towns towards growing suburbs, like Broughton,

Rusholme, Didsbury or Victoria Park, or even to Lytham, Bowdon or Altrincham, aided by the growing railway system. The line from Manchester to the Cheshire towns was opened in 1849. The Lancashire middle-class groups found some unity in an effective campaign, based largely on passive resistance, against the New Poor Law of 1834. Few of the industrial towns had workhouses functioning on the new principle for many years after 1834.

THE ANTI-CORN LAW LEAGUE

The Manchester Chamber of Commerce, which had not worried unduly about the corn laws when trade was good, was stage by stage converted to outright opposition to the latter between the depression of 1837 and the end of 1838. In the autumn, the Manchester Anti-Corn Law Association, the precursor of the nationally famous League, was formed under the leadership of Archibald Prentice, a veteran radical. Prentice's own *History of the Anti-Corn Law League* (1853) is a salute to the historic middle-class movement which was now emerging.

The League, formed in March 1839, was a brilliantly organised national movement using modern campaign methods—floods of printed propaganda and paid lecturers working tactically throughout the country—together with the resources of the new rail transport and the newer penny post (1839). The London to Manchester line was opened in 1840, and the Grand Junction Railway connecting Manchester with Wigan, Warrington and Chester had already been completed in 1837. Routes direct from the great city to Leeds, and to Carlisle, were to be opened in 1846. But even such a remarkable conjunction of events would have meant little without the great wealth of the Lancashire manufacturers who poured money into the League.

Without this wealth, even the unique partnership of Cobden and Bright would have achieved far less. The League, meanwhile, found most of its Lancashire support in the southern towns, and Blackburn, Liverpool, Wigan and Clitheroe were little influenced by it. As Cobden himself put it, Manchester '... was a good cradle for the League, for there were strong purses, and their owners thought they would be replenished by Free Trade. It was one aristocracy pitted against another . . .' (1857). After the repeal of the Corn Laws in 1846, Manchester never again offered such national leadership, and Liberalism found much of its strength elsewhere. Bright's courageous opposition to the Crimean War brought him almost total isolation.

THE LIBERAL ECLIPSE

Although the League had had some operative support in most of the Lancashire towns, both Cobden and Bright were remembered —and not only by Chartists—for their opposition to the Factory Acts. The Ten Hour Movement had brought together working men and Tory radicals, and the relative prosperity of the fifties and sixties, interrupted by the catastrophe of the Cotton Famine in 1861–3, produced a change in the temper of Lancashire working-class politics. The Lancashire mill-worker emerged as a man of complexities; a trade unionist who had little time for the meanness of his (often) Liberal employer, a drinking man who disliked the latter's (frequent) temperance tracts, a sportsman who liked open-handed gentry and despised non-conformist killjoys, and a chauvinist who detested Irish settlers and supposed Popish or Fenian influence. The 1867 Reform Act, Disraeli's leap in the dark, revealed a mass of Conservative support in the town working-class populations, and the general elections of 1868 and 1874 brought serious defeats for Lancashire Liberalism.

Large sections of the middle class had in any case forsaken the towns, to enter into 'spiritual' if opulent isolation in the newer suburbs, or geographical isolation, usually in retirement, at St Anne's (developed following 1875), or Lytham or Southport. Those who remained to take civic office did so from a carriage-journey distance, and their local pride was too often a thing concerned with externals as their redbrick semi-mansions became scattered through the lanes of Fulwood, developed as a Freehold Land Society project after 1849 for the benefit of middle-class Prestonians or, in the case of Bolton, in the leafy fastnesses of Heaton. Most of Oldham's middle-class leaders had quit the older parts of the town during the 1860s, and the Liverpool rich spread themselves coastwise.

In the case of Oldham and other towns, the growth of limited companies following the Act of 1862 meant that the mills themselves were no longer run by families of owners, but by professional managers on behalf of distant shareholders. The mill-owners with their houses overlooking a factory colony were becoming part of the Lancashire past and, as Haslam Mills of the *Manchester Guardian* put it, limited liability 'devitalised the soil' of the county. Suburbia took over, and even the richest and most stylish Liverpudlians found themselves to be mere provincials as the railway system strengthened the social dominance of London. Cobden and Bright had been able to claim a victory over the south for their Manchester men, but the south won in the end.

Civic pride remained immensely powerful, and the claims of Lancashire's industrial leaders have their monuments in Rochdale Town Hall (1870-1), Bolton's even more splendid specimen (1868-76), and Manchester's memorable one (1877). It is fitting, if sadly so, that these splendid buildings appeared in the decade of the greatest success for sanitary reform, when after a long and halting struggle, costing hundreds of thousands of lives, the Lancashire death rate began to fall. In the less fortunate towns of the county, like Burnley, the death rate (well over 30 in the 1,000) remained a disgrace, and fell to 23 in 1884. Sections of the middle class had been too ready to side-step the dangers of town life by removing their skill and knowledge. Even religious influence and conviction, a driving force earlier in the century, flagged and became less divisive as the wealthy leaders left the great town chapels to live elsewhere.

However, it would be a mistake to imagine that 'subtopia' as we now know it had arrived. The middle-class suburbs still stood among green fields, and there were great areas of farmland and moor between the towns of the Manchester-Oldham-Rochdale complex. Indeed, the rich often travelled far, and after 1896 came the 'club trains' from Blackpool, Ansdell and Lytham to Manchester, carrying business passengers during breakfast in luxury.

Lancashire's industrial and middle-class leaders were altogether more educated by the end of the century. Their fathers and grandfathers were often men of little education; the industrial dynasties were now producing university-educated men or even sportsmen, like A. N. Hornby, Lancashire's cricket captain, whose family had made its fortune at the Brookhouse mills, Blackburn. Lancashire's own assertion of cultural identity—in an academic sense—is reflected in the establishment of Owens College in Manchester in the mid-nineteenth century, and in its development into the university there (1904), and in that of the University of Liverpool between Victoria's two jubilees. More important still, perhaps, were the new technical colleges which educated Lancashire's lesser middle-class leaders, and which appeared after 1890 often as the outgrowths of mechanics' institutes.

SOURCES OF INFORMATION

There are plenty of incidental studies throwing light on the Lancashire middle class. Donald Read's *Peterloo* (1958) sketches its emergence in Manchester, and the political and social achievement of the manufacturers at the height of their influence is reflected in N. McCord, *History of the Anti-Corn Law League* (1958) and in Prentice's history mentioned in the text. Much fascinating light is thrown on the subject by John Vincent, *The Formation of the Liberal Party 1857–1868* (1966), as also by H. J. Hanham, *Elections and Party Management* (1959). Haslam Mills, *Sir Charles W. Macara, Bart,* (1917) illuminates the later nineteenth century. The reader will enjoy Katherine Chorley, *Manchester Made Them* (1950), while Orchard, *Liverpool's Legion of Honour* (1889) is an astonishing social survey of the leaders of that city. Bowker, *Lancashire Under The Hammer* (1928) provides a postscript. Dr David Foster kindly supplied the information about magistrates.

Chapter 9   LIFE IN VICTORIAN
LANCASHIRE

THE NATURE OF CHANGE

As the cotton towns grew steadily during the Victorian age, so there were great changes in the life within them. Work in the mill became even more intense, but hours were shorter, and holidays came somewhat more often. One's children had more chance of survival, and education steadily reduced illiteracy of both sexes. Most working people were better off materially, especially in the middle years of the reign, although there was still much privation.

Yet people lived in a grimly drab environment, there was much industrial conflict (the most savage trade union battles belong to this age), and there was much religious and nationalistic animosity, especially against the Irish. People tended to be satisfied with crude and simple pleasures, and life centred on the public house. Nevertheless, this was also the age of 'respectability', which term signified not only a donkey-stoned doorstep and window-sills but also money in the friendly society or co-op, and perhaps even a small share in a mill or ownership of a few terrace houses. Idealistic views of political change, like those of the Chartists, were submerged for a time, to re-appear near the end of the century as the defects of this industrial society became apparent to the thinking man and woman. The rather self-satisfied drinking Tory working man, or his cautious or critical Liberal counterpart, sometimes gave way to the Social Democratic Federation (SDF) or Independent Labour Party (ILP) supporter, and later the Labour campaigner, especially in east Lancashire.

THE QUALITY OF LIFE

As we have seen, the traditional Lancashire holidays were originally undermined by the factory system, and the mill-hand had little leisure for amusement. As hours were reduced, the public house became an ever more important social centre. There was a great surge of beerhouse opening after the Beer Act of 1830; between 1830 and 1834, 190 beerhouses were set up in Preston. In 1883, Anthony Hewitson counted 448 drinking places in the same borough, but only 228 of these were backstreet beerhouses. There were rather over 200 members of the local population to each 'pub' or beerhouse, men, women and children. Busy Burnley had about 300 places at which liquor could be obtained by the middle of Victoria's reign, or one to fewer than a hundred of its people.

The 'pub' was both a social and a political centre. Although its politics were often Tory (for the Liberals became associated with temperance), trade unions and friendly societies met in its upper rooms. Hence the Burnley branch of the Amalgamated Society of Engineers—now the Amalgamated Engineering Federation (AEF) met at the Sun Inn, and the carpenters Amalgamated Society of Carpenters and Joiners (ASC & J) met at the Hall Inn, the Albion and the St Leger. The Oddfellows would often meet in pubs, and by 1873, Lancashire had more than a quarter of all the friendly society members in England, and by far the most branches or societies of any English county—although some, like the Rechabites, were temperance bodies. In these organisations, the Lancastrian administered his own social security. Even wages were paid out in pubs in some occupations; many a drunkard traced his downward course to this custom, attacked in lurid terms by the temperance men. 'How could I help it,' said a navvy, 'I have had to wait so long at the Angel for my wages.' Other forms of business were more innocuous, and publicans encouraged shoe, clothes, hat, lottery, raffle, furniture, clock and watch clubs in order to attract custom. Later in the century, pub 'going-off clubs', designed to enable savers to prepare for their holidays in Blackpool or elsewhere, were to be counted in hundreds in the cotton towns.

The pubs were the home of a peoples' culture. Many of them, by the sixties, had a singing saloon which was really the precursor of the music hall. In the sixties, Preston's Old Cock Inn had 'excellent singing and a brass band'. In others, both sexes intermingled, there was a good fire and a piano. The Fleece Inn at Bolton, still there on Bradshawgate, even had a shooting gallery in 1855. But penny song books, increasingly circulated in the fifties and sixties, helped the Lancastrian to make his own entertainment, and singing clubs and even choirs met in public houses. This was an age of the increasing popularity of the brass band, and both cotton mills and town societies acquired them. The Besses o' th' Barn Band of Whitefield, part of Lancashire musical history,was one of the earliest to take advantage of the piston instruments of Adolphe Saxe, this in 1853. Town brass-band contests were popular by the sixties, and the railways helped to widen their influence.

THE TEMPERANCE STRUGGLE

In view of Preston's massive concentration of drinking establishments, it seems hardly surprising that an important teetotal movement originated there. Although Joseph Livesey, former weaver of Walton-le-Dale, was the moving force, the word was stammered out passionately by his lieutenant, 'Dicky' Turner, a reformed drunkard as 'tee-total' abstinence. This slip of the tongue became the property of the English-speaking world (1832), and the movement spread as widely.

The movement was at first a rebel and radical one; only later did it become wholly respectable, so that nationally a section of the Anglicans (1862) adopted temperance, as did a group of Catholics in 1872. Although relations between Anglicans and dissenters had been strained in most towns, the common enemy of drunkenness drew them closer together. Mass rallies were common by mid-Victorian times, and the Band of Hope was a feature of most places. The numbers of 'pubs' show that most Lancastrians preferred their beer. As the Lancashire song put it, through the mouth of the mill-worker, 'Ale is physic for me.' Attempts to control drinking and pubs, associated with Mr Gladstone's party in the 1860s and 1870s, did much damage to the Liberal cause. Open drunkenness was still rife, especially on Saturday nights, at the end of the century.

THE REFORM OF TOWN LIFE

The reform of town life and conditions did not come about merely through bigger, better and more representative local boards and councils; the removal of newspaper taxes in the 1850s led to a vast increase of reading matter and local press influence. The weekly newspaper of the 1850s had given place to daily or even evening papers by the time of Victoria's Golden Jubilee (1887), at Barrow, Blackburn, Bolton (where there was an evening paper in 1873), and at Oldham, Preston and Rochdale (where there was such a paper in 1870). Circulations increased twenty-fold from a few hundred or thousands, and the spread of literacy, a steady process which had its roots in the period before the Education Act of 1870, is remarkable testimony to the stimulus which newspapers gave as well as to the work of ill-paid teachers in church, chapel and board schools.

It should be borne in mind that the average Lancashire figures traced in Fig 11 have the effect of masking the backwardness of some industrial towns like Blackburn, which had only half as many teachers *per capita* as the county average (1871). Lancashire women, as can be seen, suffered serious disadvantage compared with those throughout the country generally. These figures, for what they are worth (and they relate only to people who could not sign marriage registers), still tell a much more significant story than any conventional history of local education. It is a complex story; the Irish pulled down standards in some places, and girl employment in others, and there is much to be discovered.

The Victorian local press, although generally dedicated to the support of the existing social system, could be far more ruthlessly critical of public persons than the local press of today, inhibited as it is by the use of the law of libel to protect the privileged. The literate working man could read what was said about his betters,

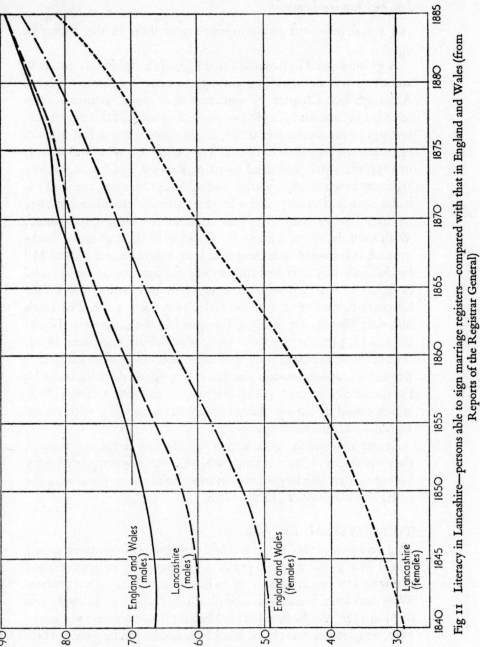

Fig 11 Literacy in Lancashire—persons able to sign marriage registers—compared with that in England and Wales (from Reports of the Registrar General)

and a real informed public opinion was born in the Victorian age.

A ground-swell of demand for things of the spirit was not new, and there was a real culture among the early handloom weavers. Although (see Chapter 7) numerous mechanics' institutes were founded in Lancashire in 1824-5, the real upsurge of this movement belongs to the forties and fifties, when most of the urban districts of Lancashire had such institutes. The public was wide and varied; in 1854, the small industrial town of Royton had 'in its vicinity eighteen newsrooms, libraries and self-improvement societies'. It had a botanical society, and a literary institute 'established in 1848 by nine factory lads who were anxious for self-improvement'. With such depths of passion for learning in the mill-town background, it is hardly surprising that Joseph Brotherton, radical MP for Salford, was able to bring to life the first public library and museum in that borough in 1850. This was before the Public Libraries Act of 1850, but the latter stimulated a series of town libraries: Manchester in 1852, Liverpool in the same year, Blackburn in 1853 (the library there was not actually opened until 1860), Bolton about the same time, and other textile towns much later— Burnley's culture through the book was guarded successively by the mechanics' institute (1834) and the co-operative society (1860), which closed its Co-operative Library as late as 1925, with 10,000 volumes and nine reading rooms.

Examples from the great towns suggest that about one-third of the early readers were working men, although it was reported from Liverpool that 'the larger proportion of solid reading is among the really working classes', in the 1860s.

THE PHYSICAL ESCAPE

Men and sometimes women could also escape from their grimy world in a physical sense; parks were beginning to appear amid the wastes of brick, mortar or millstone grit. Preston's Avenham Walk had long been a place of pleasure. Peel Park, Salford, was open in 1846, the former Larkhill Estate; it had 600,000 visitors in 1850, 800,000 ten years later. Blackburn had its public park in 1857, but nearby Burnley had to wait until 1872, when Healey Heights were bought by the corporation. Blackburn's Corporation Park was improved during the Cotton Famine, and Bolton's Queen's Park was commenced at that time, to receive its present name at the Golden Jubilee in 1887. Blackburn's Queen's Park, similarly named, was nearer to the steep streets on the eastern side of the town, and was accordingly a blessing. Oldham's Swine Clough Park was another creation of the Cotton Famine period.

There was plenty to escape from. The slums of course remained for the most part, but Victoria's middle years saw also the rise of a determined respectability among the skilled workers and over-lookers, marked by houses kept aggressively clean despite the filth that showered from the mill chimneys. Bolton, in its hollow beneath Smithills Moor, was under a permanent pall of smoke, and only the present smoke control and closing of the mills has made it clearly visible from that viewpoint. A municipal tram system, which could carry people far away to the outskirts of the great towns, was not adequately developed until the arrival of the electric trams of Edwardian times.

Great reservoirs now glistened about the Pennine foothills. They had supplied town water—from Rivington (for Liverpool), Belmont (for Bolton), Heckenhurst (for Burnley) or Longdendale (for Manchester)—for a lifetime or near it by the end of Victoria's reign, and most Lancastrians had become used to 'corporation pop' spiced with disinfectant. It had been possible to use public baths for about as long, and Bolton's baths building (1846)—a 'Grecian building of stone, very capacious and used as an assembly room for lectures and exhibitions'—is still there on Bridgeman Place. It had bathing facilities for ladies, gentlemen and workmen. Oldham, Preston and Burnley provided public baths by private subscription in the 1840s. The corollary, that terrace houses had no bath, remained true until the twentieth century.

There was another way of cleansing oneself; the proceeds from the going-off club payments could be used to take the worker to hugely growing Blackpool by cheap train ticket for three or four days, with a tin trunk of food and clothing, there to look after

95

family needs in a lodging (though not boarding) house, crowded and barely furnished.

What the Lancastrian sought at Blackpool, which had its imitation Eiffel Tower by 1894 and its Big Wheel in 1897, reflected his tastes in music hall elsewhere. Most of the Lancashire towns had long had theatres, but the eighties and nineties brought the music halls so that Burnley, after several theatres, got its Empire Music Hall (1894). Manchester had three music halls by 1902, Preston had its Gaiety Theatre in 1882, and Blackburn its New Palace Theatre by 1899.

The eighties also brought another significant addition to social and recreational life, with the development and professionalisation of sport, especially association football. Both cricket and football had long been part of the Lancashire scene, although the former was restricted socially and the latter much hampered by the enclosure of open spaces in early Victorian times. Both sports benefited from the increased Saturday leisure available to the artisan by the seventies, although a century of spectator-sport was thereby on its way; this was the mass world of the watcher as well as the player. Yet 'looking on' was not new, and the main mass sports of the earlier nineteenth century, wrestling and cockfighting, were of this type.

By the eighties, great clubs like Manchester City FC (which started in 1880 as West Gorton FC) and Manchester United were in being. Burnley appeared in 1883 as a product of the local cricket club, and Blackburn Rovers, Bolton Wanderers, Blackpool and Preston North End were all on their way to fame. The Lancashire County Cricket Club was founded in 1864 and, driven by the boundless energy of the Hornby family, had achieved fame by the eighties and more than that to multitudes at Old Trafford (as the writings of Sir Neville Cardus will always remind us) by the time of the accession of Edward VII. Cricket was a great mass watcher-sport by that time, but it was acquiring its thousands of players, and the North East Lancashire League was founded in 1891. The *Victoria County History for Lancashire*, evidently written for gentlemen by gentlemen (1906) does not mention 'soccer', but it does mention flat racing and steeplechasing (the Grand National at Aintree was inaugurated in 1839), and it describes golf without even hinting at the social significance of the appearance of golf clubs and courses at Birkdale (1889), Blackpool (1894), Ansdell (1895) and Hesketh (1902).

To swing, sharply, to another end of the social scale. It is known that fish and chip frying commenced in Oldham after 1880; ranges for the purpose had been made there before that, and the invention is not a Lancashire one. Specialised fish and chip shops were in Blackpool by Edwardian times, and modern Lancashire had its favourite food.

SOME SOURCES OF INFORMATION

An article by Mr M. B. Smith, 'Victorian Music Hall Entertainment in the Lancashire Cotton Towns', will be found in *The Local Historian* (vol 9, no 8, 1971). The town histories already listed (Chapter 4) provide some useful information, as does Miss Kathleen Eyre's *Seven Golden Miles* (1961). To these may be added Anthony Hewitson's *History of Preston*, a remarkable Victorian compendium by a local journalist. For fundamental generalisations, one must search such sources as the *Transactions of the Manchester Statistical Society*, the *Journal of the (Royal) Statistical Society*, and the annual *Reports of the Registrar-General*. All of these are in the Manchester Reference Library. I wish to thank Mr I. R. Cowan, Mr J. K. Walton and Dr W. H. Chaloner for items in this chapter. S. Peter Bell (ed) *Victorian Lancashire* (1974) adds much specialised information to topics discussed in this chapter.

Chapter 10   THE INDUSTRIES OF
LANCASHIRE, 1850–1914

KING COTTON

IN 1851, there were rather over half a million cotton workers in Great Britain, counting printers and dyers, and of these, two-thirds were in Lancashire. At the end of the century, the proportion was still much the same. In its middle years, there had been a great growth in the flow of cotton goods to India, Ceylon and Turkey, to China and the newly acquired base of Hong-Kong, and to the West Indies and Brazil. Cotton goods exports were, in money values, from 30 to 40 per cent of all the exports of the United Kingdom, and even in 1912, the share of cotton was one-quarter. The home market absorbed about 15 per cent of output, and it was said that this work could be done before breakfast.

It is startling to recall that just before 1850, much of the work for this vast world market had been done on the handloom. But in the following twenty to thirty years, the numbers of powerlooms increased over fourfold, and the appearance of specialist weaving sheds and factories was accompanied by a steady growth of regional specialisation, as east Lancashire became a weaving area and other areas concerned themselves more exclusively with spinning. However, the weaving towns themselves developed characteristic products, so that the Preston-Chorley district became noted for its fine light fabrics, and towns further east, like Blackburn and Accrington, for dhooties, shirts and other goods shipped exclusively to India. In the spinning area of the county, Bolton and Manchester were noted for their fine-spun yarns (Bolton, the home of Crompton and the mule, especially so), and Oldham produced coarser weaving yarns.

Throughout the major part of the nineteenth century, rather over half of the cotton labour force consisted of women and girls. The highly skilled workers, however, were nearly always adult males, who came to see themselves as a caste apart—like the mulespinners, who often wore high collars and bowler hats and who brought their lunch to work in gladstone bags! Men like this soon came together in union organisation to protect their own sectional interests, striving to control apprenticeship to the job. The spinners were assisted by 'big' and 'little' piecers, the latter mere boys who brought their food to work in a handkerchief, but neither type of helper was at first encouraged to organise.

However, there were many other spinning processes, like carding, doubling and gassing, and the workers in these sections often became organised in small and separate unions organised on a local basis. But only a tiny proportion of all cotton workers, fewer than 10 per cent, were in the unions, nearly all of them male and split into as many as 200 local units. The weavers were more prone than the groups of spinners to collaborate in 'amalgamations' and to encourage the branches of their trade to organise. They were also the first to appoint skilled full-time union negotiators.

Official union organisation was not always a measure of the militancy of the cotton workers, whose industry produced nearly as many strikes as did coal-mining, and the middle years of the century saw many heavy conflicts in the northern or Preston-centred part of the cotton district (1848–70), and later in the Oldham-centred southern part (1878–93). The first wave of strikes occurred when mills were generally run by small or family firms, and the later ones took place when larger mills run by managers on behalf of 'faceless' shareholders were more common, especially in the Oldham district. Apart from this, the industry was bedevilled by a mass of piece rates for almost innumerable kinds of work, set out in the famous Bolton and Blackburn lists, and only tiny groups of workers and employers could claim to understand

99

these constant causes of dispute. One group could stop a whole section of the industry.

But there were underlying pressures of a different kind. There was an increase in the speed of working of both spinning machines and powerlooms. Outputs per man-hour rose steadily during much of the nineteenth century, and the number of powerlooms to be 'tented' by each minder grew from one or two to four, while the handloom weaver was virtually crushed out of existence in all but a few villages. This period of growing output was also one of fairly steady increase in factory wages and earnings from about 1850, although the Cotton Famine (1862–3), caused by the southern states' blockade of raw cotton supplies in the American Civil War, led to much privation. Profits seem not to have suffered unduly, and labour costs probably fell despite the absence of major inventions in the trade.

The employers, too, formed associations, combining locally at first in areas like Bolton and Oldham, and later federating such bodies into powerful masters' organisations. A great spinners' strike of 1892, lasting for five months, was followed by the famous 'Brooklands Agreement' of 1893, which set up a system of industrial courts for a time.

Despite foreign competition and the recessions of the eighties and nineties, the Lancashire cotton industry remained powerful and competitive until 1914. An all-time export record for cotton was reached in 1913, and many new mills, some of them using the new-fangled ring-spindle and the Northrop loom, were built between 1903 and 1913. These structures, with their terra-cotta facing, cathedral-like engine-houses and lofty towers with names like India Mill or Atlas Mill, are still features of the landscape.

SOME ASSOCIATED INDUSTRIES

Cotton goods were not of course merely spun or woven, and the dyeing, bleaching and finishing industries of Lancashire were important too. Bleaching accounted for about 5 per cent of the total cotton labour force, and was traditionally strong near Bolton, where firms like Slaters, Ainsworths and Hardcastles dated from the eighteenth century. With bleaching went dyeing, originally done with vegetable dyes, and printing by rollers. Calico-printing was a fairly important industry in the east of the county. The development of aniline dyes by W. H. Perkin, set on an industrial basis by him in the 1860s, was finally concentrated in the Manchester district. After 1900, the selection of synthetic colours increased a hundredfold.

The silk industry of Lancashire was of some consequence until the later nineteenth century, when it dwindled to a small remnant in the Leigh district. Woollens and flannel remained traditional products in Rochdale, and there was a famous felt-hat industry in south-east Lancashire, and in the Stockport area, which was revived in late Victorian times to make trilby hats.

MAKING THE MACHINES

Textile machinery making grew up in Lancashire, which had produced such equipment since the days of Crompton, when Dobson & Barlow of Bolton constructed mules. This great firm, together with Mather & Platts of Salford and Platt Brothers of Oldham, went on to make cotton machinery for international markets. The next step was to make 'machines to make machines', ie machine tools, and Richard Roberts, who invented the self-acting spinning mule in 1825, was a pioneer in this field. Roberts & Co later produced parts not only for textile machinery but also for locomotives. Joseph Whitworth, another Lancashire-based engineer, made a vast contribution by his development of Maudslay's idea of the standardisation of screw threads, and he had a works at Openshaw in 1880. From 1836, James Nasmyth (who invented the steam hammer in 1839) laid the foundation for modern works organisation and production-flow techniques at Patricroft near Eccles.

Both Roberts and Nasmyth were pioneering locomotive builders, although firms like Galloways of Knott Mill; Rothwell, Hick & Rothwell of Bolton; and Beyer & Peacock (1854) were the ones to gain international repute in this industry. The Lancashire railway network stimulated inventiveness from the time of the

Bolton & Leigh Railway of 1828, which set Hick & Rothwell in action. (The story of the Liverpool & Manchester Railway, 1830, is well known.)

RAILWAYS AND COAL

The main outlines of Lancashire's railway system had appeared between 1830 and 1850, when the main north-south lines were already completed. The network of the East Lancashire Railway had connected Blackburn, Burnley and Colne, helping the power weavers to specialise in those towns. Meanwhile, the line making a circuit of the Fylde, and first of all connecting Preston and Fleetwood, was completed in this period and, very soon, an outflow of visitors was making its way to Blackpool and Lytham. The 'commuter' territory of Southport and district was developed from Liverpool's railway connection up the coast, but this was mainly after 1850. The great railway companies, later in the century, developed railway works and communities at Earlestown (LNWR), Horwich (L & Y) and Gorton (MSLR). Horwich in particular became a flourishing company town.

The local canals, and then the railway lines, took coal into ever-growing Liverpool and Manchester, but the Lancashire industrial towns in general had coal upon their doorsteps, and the railways were more valuable as general carriers. The extensive and fragmented Lancashire coalfield had hundreds of small coalpits which supplied nearby mills. There were some deep, large collieries in south Lancashire, but conditions throughout tended to be crude and primitive, and the Wigan miner in particular was noted for his roughness. The region was backward, even in trade unionism, although there were advances by the 1880s. Pit-brow lassies remained part of Wigan life.

Coal-mining was decisive in its economic effects in south-west Lancashire, where the chemical industries of Widnes and St Helens required coal and salt, and where the St Helens glass industry had need of coal and soda ash.

OTHER INDUSTRIES

Mention should be made of the great Furness iron and steel industry which stimulated the rise of Barrow, and of the enormous transformation of that district between 1850 and 1880. Here the Furness railway played a vital role in carrying coke and iron-ore and iron. But the great dreams of the Barrow ironmasters were never fully realised, and Barrow docks remained partly unused. Wigan, meanwhile, had its iron as well as its coal industry.

Paper was made in numerous mills on the rivers Irwell and Darwen; pins, files and hardware, as well as chemicals, were made at Warrington; and the Prescot district remained a centre for watch parts. There was a considerable inshore fishing industry, catching shrimps, prawns and mussels in Morecambe Bay and coastal Lancashire. Deep-sea trawling was based on Fleetwood, but scarcely more than 2,000 men were employed in these industries by Edwardian times.

The Manchester district saw the most significant changes of all at the end of the century. The age of electricity and steel began to challenge that of steam and iron. Mather & Platts, the famous textile engineers, became electrical engineers from the 1880s, and the British Westinghouse Electrical & Manufacturing Company (later Metrovicks) established a works in Trafford Park in 1900-2. The twentieth century had begun in a very real sense. Manchester had earlier made its historic bid for great port status by building the Manchester Ship Canal (1885-93) at a cost of some £17,000,000.

THE RURAL ECONOMY IN MODERN TIMES

The emphasis—in Lancashire's story as told in these pages—has been very much on towns and town industries. The Lancashire countryside, from the early eighteenth century, was supplying its towns with people; yet its farmers remained numerous, and were often workers in textiles as well.

The growth of towns created huge demands for vegetables, fodder, milk, meat and cereals, especially oats. Much of this food had to come from other counties, but much was grown in Lancashire. Hence, the expansion of Liverpool led to the appearance of a huge market-gardening area within a few miles of the town and, beyond that, at a distance of ten miles or so, a ring of dairy and arable farms, the latter producing potatoes and fodder. Oats, potatoes, carrots and green vegetables were grown along the line of the Leeds & Liverpool and Bridgwater canals, both important waterways in the early days of industrialisation.

Farther north, the Fylde and Furness areas were (from the 1750s) the granaries of the county, and in Furness and north Lancashire the farming—under the stimulus of great landowners like the Dukes of Devonshire—was quite advanced by the mid-nineteenth century. Other major landowners in plainland Lancashire, like the Cliftons of Lytham, the Heskeths of Rufford, and the Earls of Derby, promoted land reclamation or so-called high farming. Generally, however, the countryside was dominated by the small farmer or small yeoman-landowner.

In the eastern foothills of the county, the small occupiers there were backward by comparison, knowing little about crop rotations or root crops like turnips, and understandably given to concentrating on sheep and cattle. But where growing towns gave them a market, then they experimented and sometimes became better suppliers of dairy products and meat.

Perhaps the most remarkable achievement of Lancashire agriculture in modern times, to be credited chiefly to great landowners, was the drainage and reclamation of the mosses (or swamps) from the eighteenth century: Trafford Moss, Chat Moss, Marton Moss and Pilling Moss in the north. But small men also played their part, although they lacked capital to undertake large-scale drainage using tiles and trenches. The enclosure movement of Lancashire, from about 1760, was also concerned with reclamation, not only of mosses, but also of moorland and waste. It is important to know this, because local enclosure did *not* drive people from the land in great numbers (as is often said about enclosures generally), because it brought more land into production.

People left the land for a great variety of reasons: sheer poverty, poor housing, winter unemployment (common in arable districts), the need to find jobs for children, and the restlessness caused by hearing from friends and relatives in the towns, are among the major ones. In fact, Lancashire villages only began to *decline* in total population in the middle of last century. Previous to that time, high birth rates and lowish death rates had always produced more country people than the countryside could support, but a large number of these surplus folk left for the towns, leaving a more slowly growing rural population. The effect of towns and industries generally was to force wages up in the nearby countryside, and wages in Lancashire agriculture were among the highest in England. The continued growth of nineteenth-century Lancashire population helped Lancashire agriculture to survive the enormous competition of grain and meat from Canada or New Zealand; milk, meat and dairy produce or vegetables could be sold to town-dwellers, and so there was no real 'depression' in farming after the late 1870s.

This emphasis on livestock and dairying, or specialised market gardening, has remained and even spread. The vast demands of Blackpool stimulate glasshouses and poultry farming in the Fylde. Roughly half of Lancashire's 16,000 farms are concerned with dairying. Beef cattle have traditionally been reared on the rich pastures of the Lancashire valleys and the lower foothills, and farmers with access to fell or mossland keep sheep. In the plainland and valleys, much land is cultivated for roots and fodder, and oats and maincrop potatoes are widely grown in west Lancashire, following a centuries-old tradition.

POPULATION CHANGES

Although the Lancashire population continued to grow at rates faster than those for England and Wales, there were important and sometimes ominous variations within the county during this period. The rural townships were losing people, 1851–81, to the point of absolute decline, and many of the older towns and industrial areas, especially in the textile districts, were growing more slowly than in the early nineteenth century, largely because birth rates were beginning to fall.

But natural increase (excess of births over deaths) remained high throughout the whole of the north-west. As the centres of the great cities lost population, so the Liverpool and Manchester suburban areas gained it in the late nineteenth century and early twentieth. However, there was a sharp fall in natural increase in the textile towns after 1881, and there was also a drain of Lancashire people away to other parts of England. Yet much of this was only a redressing of the balance, as against the enormous earlier gain in migrants, including Irish ones, and south Lancashire remained one of the most thickly populated areas in the world. Its suburbanisation was in reality only commencing.

SOME READING

There are some valuable books on the Lancashire cotton industry; one of the most useful is S. J. Chapman's book of that title (1904), while T. Ellison's *Cotton Trade of Great Britain* (1882) has now been reprinted. A more recent study is L. H. C. Tippett's *A Portrait of the Lancashire Textile Industry* (1969). On working problems and trade union matters, the main work of reference is H. A. Turner's *Trade Union Growth, Structure and Policy* (1962), which is concerned with the cotton unions.

Industries in general are surveyed in O. Ashmore, *The Industrial Archaeology of Lancashire* (1969), which has an excellent bibliography as well as detailed information on all the industries mentioned in this chapter, and there is briefer but authoritative material in J. H. Smith (ed), '*The Great Human Exploit' : Historic Industries of the North-West* (1973). The sections on Lancashire industries in vol 2 of the *Victoria County History of Lancashire* are often most useful. On railways, a thorough bibliography will be found in Mr Ashmore's book, but O. S. Nock's *The Lancashire and Yorkshire Railway; A Concise History* (1969) can be added to it, and also contains some interesting regional sidelights. Mr John Marshall's *Lancashire and Yorkshire Railway* (2 vols 1969–70) is very detailed. (He is no relative of the present writer.)

Further social information of a revealing kind is to be found in R. C. Challinor, *The Lancashire and Cheshire Miners* (1972). On population, Professor R. Lawton's 'Population Trends in Lancashire and Cheshire from 1801', in *Transactions of the Historic Society of Lancashire and Cheshire*, vol 114, 1962, is a most helpful summary.

Chapter 11   GOVERNMENT OF THE
COUNTY: SIXTEENTH TO
TWENTIETH CENTURY

FROM Tudor times nearly to the end of the
nineteenth century, the county of Lancashire was governed by
justices of the peace (magistrates) operating through Quarter
Sessions held four times a year at convenient centres like Manchester, Wigan, Liverpool, Preston and Lancaster. But, as more
and more towns became municipal boroughs and had their own
government, so the country gentry, who had it all their own way
until Victoria came to the throne, and who made up a large
proportion of the justices, had their influence challenged by the
industrial middle class in the towns. But some of these, in turn,
tended to become rural or suburban gentry.

Meanwhile, the problems of the county as a whole multiplied.
Its population increased some 413 per cent between 1801 and 1881.
During that time, its death rates were higher (in some cases, as in
Liverpool and Manchester, much higher) than the national
average, it was more subject to epidemics than most other counties,
and in so far as it is safe to trust the committal statistics of the time,
it had more crime. It had too few cemeteries, too few sewers in
town and country, and too few teachers and policemen.

Both the gentry and the property-owning industrialists were
concerned with the police and their control. Between Elizabeth's
reign and 1839 the keeping of the peace devolved largely on parish
constables, but in November 1839 it was decided to establish a
County Police Force following the Constabulary Act of that year.
The force was at first short of good recruits and was ill-

administered. Meanwhile eleven Lancashire boroughs established, with some difficulty, police forces by 1856, some of them doing so because their local leaders suspected the gentry-ruled county organisation. This 'split' remained to the present century.

The magistracy's rule was weakened, however, when the care of the county and parish poor (with which it had been charged since 1601) was taken out of its hands and placed in those of the Board of Guardians following Chadwick's famous Act of 1834 (the Poor Law Amendment Act). This new system did more than build the 'Oliver Twist' style union workhouse, some of which are now hospitals, like the Stanley Hospital at Ulverston. It provided some medical care, schooling and sanitary control. Its more degrading aspects, however, were hotly opposed in east Lancashire between 1834 and 1840—the system of 'less eligibility' attempted to make poverty contemptible and subject to punishment, and the workhouse came to carry an evil stigma which has never been forgotten.

Despite some long and successful opposition, thirty-two town and country Poor Law Unions became operative in Lancashire, with elected Guardians, eventually providing a large range of services (hospitals, maternity homes, sanatoria) until their function was taken over by the county and county boroughs in 1929.

TOWN GOVERNMENT

The other major problems, beyond those of policing and poverty, were tackled seriously only after the 1860s, when most Lancashire towns by degrees dealt with filth, disease and refuse disposal. Only Manchester and Liverpool had medical officers of health by 1868, and some Lancashire town councils showed themselves to be as concerned with lighting and market control as they were with water and sewers. Even in 1874, Wigan had no uniform system of sewerage, and Bolton had been equally slow to deal with sewage disposal. Yet Lancashire had twenty-six municipal boroughs, and no fewer than ninety-eight local boards of health, covering semi-urban and urban districts as well as country ones, by 1886; so the framework for real improvement existed. Most of the local boards appeared during and after the 1850s.

The Public Health Acts of 1872 and 1875, the working of which was directed by the Local Government Board (1871), gave real teeth to sanitary improvement, and resulted in the establishment of urban and rural sanitary districts. The former were in the great majority of cases the old local boards, and they usually became the urban district councils (formed in 1894) of the present day, with minor variations. The rural sanitary districts were based on the Poor Law Unions, and they did little to improve rural water supplies or sanitation. Meanwhile, the towns effected, in most cases, a drop in their death rates by the 1880s and 1890s. Houses were built under strict regulation, at last, following the provisions of the 1875 Public Health Act, and the first real battle against muck was won.

Town government has altered in scale, rather than character, since those days (despite the advent of class-political conflict from the 1890s), and it provides a much wider range of welfare and other services. Nevertheless, essential transformations have been slow, and south Lancashire is still short of housing. The Wheatley Act of 1919 led to the building of council estates and the great Lancashire towns like Bolton, built largely: Bolton put up over 4,000 'council' dwellings between 1919 and 1939. But effective slum clearance came only after 1945 in most areas, creating an even greater housing problem in the county at large. The establishment of a new town at Skelmersdale has had to provide a part-solution, and the 'Hanky Park' of *Love on the Dole* has almost totally disappeared from Salford, as flats have arisen instead.

Meanwhile, the vast twentieth-century suburban spread, far exceeding that of the 'insensate towns' of the Industrial Revolution, has been largely unplanned. The muck, too, has stayed in the same places, and the money has gone to Southport or Lytham St Anne's.

THE COUNTY COUNCIL
Who is to blame for unplanned housing or other development over a very large area? Until 1889, there was no overriding authority for the county as a whole, although there had been a county administration from the Middle Ages, and by degrees

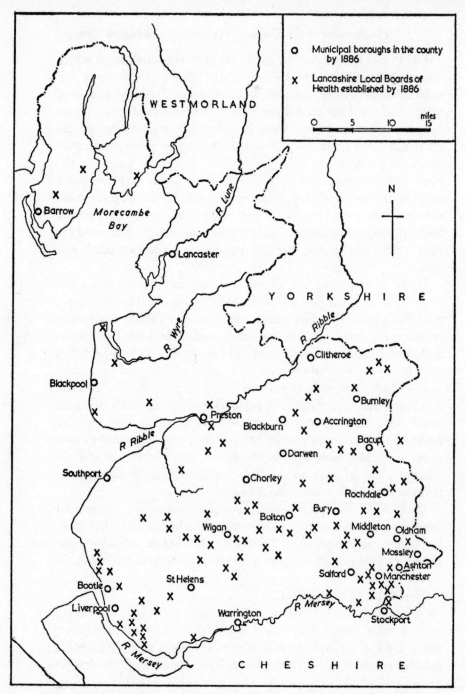

Fig 12   Public health in Lancashire: the first successful battle against dirt and death

this came to be concerned with bridges and highways, gaols, the militia, weights and measures, lunatic asylums and the police, as well as certain courts. The work of the justices has been mentioned.

But the justices were nominees of the Crown (through, in Lancashire, the Duchy of Lancaster), and it was felt to be time to run such great areas through *elected* representatives. In many counties, like neighbouring Cheshire, the election principle made little difference, and the country gentry, who provided the magistrate class, reigned as before. In Lancashire, a council consisting substantially of industrial leaders and business people (many of whom were a new magistracy and gentry) held its first meeting in January 1889, and very slowly set about the taking over and maintenance of main roads and bridges, the supervision of public health and, a main task, the running of the county police through a Standing Joint Committee. Council representatives took part in joint committees designed to control the pollution of the rivers Ribble, Mersey and Irwell (under the terms of an anti-pollution Act of 1876). But this was only the merest beginning of the fight to control the environment. In 1904 the River Lune was found to be full of sewage from the town of Lancaster, and this was by no means the worst case in the county. The County Health Committee, meanwhile, was continually reporting outbreaks of smallpox, diphtheria and other diseases in industrial or urban areas, and it is also clear that sewering and sanitation were almost non-existent in parts of rural Lancashire, whence milk, cheese and vegetables came in quantity. The fight against unclean and adulterated food was now well organised through the county and county borough authorities and their inspectors of food and drugs.

Many of the ills of the past had stemmed from the unplanned growth of housing; yet real large-scale planning in the county and large towns did not come until the passing of the Town and Country Planning Act 1947, which provided for the extensive control of land use. One need only look at some of the semi-derelict areas in the Wigan-Atherton locality to see how urgent has been the cleaning-up problem left by Lancashire industry.

The county planning organisation is now a large one, but economic and social planning have to be discussed by other bodies (see Chapter 12). The local government of the county is in any case being totally reorganised, and the county council area is being much reduced.

EDUCATION

The Education Act of 1870 was a first real step towards the free and compulsory education of the children of the nation. Up to that time, virtually all local education had been provided by the schools erected by religious bodies. Under the Act, elected School Boards for each district might build schools in localities where no elementary education was available, and try to compel attendance at the other schools. In fact, a great many children avoided schooling for ten or twenty years afterwards. Lancashire was especially troubled by the 'part-timer', the child of ten to thirteen who could, by passing a simple examination, attend school for two and a half days a week only. This 'system' was abolished as late as 1920, and was responsible for much child labour in the factories, although many Lancashire textile employers and unions tended to support it until the present century, when attitudes became more enlightened.

Although the larger towns had effective School Boards, until their abolition in 1902 (and their effects are suggested by the graph on page 93), the county as a whole was short of teachers and schools, and when the County Council, under the terms of the famous Education Act of 1902, brought under its control no fewer than 700 public elementary schools outside the great towns, some of these had been unsatisfactorily run and many were inadequately built. It set about improving them, and increased the pay of its teachers. It took over technical, secondary and 'higher' education generally, outside the large boroughs, and formed no fewer than thirty-five District Committees to supervise the education in district council and parish areas. Not surprisingly, it became a massive service with, eventually, a yearly budget running into many millions of pounds. The Lancashire County Library grew up under the wing of the County Education Committee.

Not all has been plain sailing in recent years, and there has been much controversy over the secondary schools in town and country—should they take in all children, on the comprehensive principle, or should only the gifted go to the grammar schools, and the rest to the modern or technical secondary schools formed after the 1944 Education Act? Lancashire's better known privately founded grammar schools, like Bolton School and Manchester Grammar School, still enjoy great esteem. Successive Lancashire Education Committees have been influenced, until very recent years, by such examples, and the controversy is not over. Important 'comprehensive' experiments are taking place nevertheless.

FURTHER STUDY

Dr Eric Midwinter's *Social Administration in Lancashire* (1969) is one of the very few readable accounts of local government in the county, but it takes its subject to 1860 only. There is, as yet, no good published history of the County Council, although material is in preparation, and students will find masses of information in the Lancashire County Record Office. Of detailed local studies, the following give thorough accounts of local government: Barker and Harris, *A Merseyside town in the Industrial Revolution* (1959), a history of St Helens; Bennett, *History of Burnley* (vol 4, 1951); Marshall, *Furness and the Industrial Revolution* (1958); Redford and Russell, *History of Local Government in Manchester* (3 vols, 1939–40).

Chapter 12   FROM WORLD WAR I
                 TO THE PRESENT

DURING these years, the county suffered two
serious blows: the decline of the cotton industry to a seeming near-
extinction, and the parallel decline of the coalfield on which much
of the former was situated. At the same time, important new
industrial developments have given cause for hope.

Lancashire's twentieth-century troubles have been reflected in a
rate of population increase well below the national average—for
example, it was more than 3 per cent below in the decade 1951–61
—largely because young people have been leaving the older textile
towns, and the promoters of new industries have been unwilling to
establish them in these areas. But, over west and south-west
Lancashire, some vigorous industrial expansion has been taking
place, especially in light engineering and chemicals, and so the
county population is being redistributed by degrees.

KING COTTON ABDICATES
After World War I the Lancashire cotton industry suffered badly,
in that export markets in cotton piece goods were captured by
other countries: Great Britain lost nearly one-third of the total
volume of world trade in these exports between 1913 and 1929.
Then Japan, a powerful low-cost competitor, took away much
remaining trade in the thirties. World War II, with its demands on
space and labour for arms production, gave the industry yet
another blow. Tens of thousands of expert mule-spinners were
never again to return to the mills, and an industry with masses of

obsolete machinery had to face the post-war world and stern competition from Asian countries.

The Cotton Industry Act of 1960 provided for the reorganisation of the industry by modernising some mills and closing others, and scrapping the obsolete machinery, paying compensation to the owners where appropriate. The old mules went to the scrapyard in thousands, but the new ring-spinning machinery came late to many mills, and such equipment had to be kept in operation day and night to make it really pay. There was the greater difficulty of modernising the weaving sections.

And who was to supervise the machines on night shift? The old mule-spinners had largely gone, and the ring-spinners were women who certainly would not work beyond the evening. The situation has been saved by the use of workers from the Indian sub-continent, who are now part of the life of the Lancashire towns. Meanwhile, the industry now uses man-made fibres for many purposes, and knitting processes are replacing weaving in some sectors. The movement is now towards the domestic market and trade in branded advertised fashion goods, or sales to industrial countries.

THE COALFIELD

The Lancashire coal industry has declined somewhat less rapidly than cotton, and the coal itself is technically far from exhausted. Unfortunately, the robbing tactics of earlier days have taken the most workable and left behind many narrow and faulted seams. Dozens of small collieries have closed within the last thirty years, especially in the east Lancashire section of the field, where only a tiny handful of miners remain, and the policy of the National Coal Board has been to concentrate production at a few pits, especially at the extreme southern limit of the field.

Hence, Lancashire coal now comes up the shafts of great collieries like Bradford (Manchester), Agecroft near Pendlebury and Mosley Common. Even so, less than half of the county's needs are met by coal from such sources. Perhaps the establishment of an atomic energy plant at Heysham points the way to the future (1972).

EFFECTS ON THE TOWNS

The great Lancashire towns suffered badly from the decline of these major industries. The spinning towns of the south-east, Preston, Chorley, Bolton, Bury and Blackburn, grew in population by less than 7 per cent in the first half of the present century, and the populations of both the weaving and the spinning areas declined absolutely between the world wars.

But not all the large towns shared equally in this sad decline, and Preston, which had a great variety of industry, was enabled to adapt itself to a new industrial scene: the English Electric Company and Leyland Motors represent that scene in Lancashire. Bolton, by contrast, suffered blows not only to its fine spinning but also to its coal-mining and general engineering. Yet this town, too, has shown a remarkable resilience, and its industries have become more varied in a way typical of present-day south Lancashire, in an expansion of distributive trades, catering, entertainment and building industries, as well as clothing manufacture (Burtons) and aircraft components (de Havilland). The weaving towns of east Lancashire, and their large urban areas, suffered more severely than any in the county. In the thirty-four years before 1945, the population of Blackburn district alone declined by 32,000 people. Unfortunately, the quality of life in such an area had always suffered from its dependence on the mills, and the low standards of the nineteenth century were carried on. Burnley suffered under similar burdens.

It has not been easy to give these towns new industrial structures, and the newer economic growth sectors of Lancashire are generally in the south end south-west of the county.

THE REPLACEMENT AND ALTERNATIVE INDUSTRIES

Today, coal and cotton provide only about 15 per cent of the county's employment. Engineering and metal-working, which have deep roots in the county's history, are by far the largest givers of employment, followed by chemicals, clothing, food and paper. Neither paper nor chemicals is new to the region, but vehicle building and electrical engineering are important additions to its traditional industries. Older forms of engineering, which have declined, are the manufacture of textile machinery and railway engineering.

The empty cotton mills have often been taken over by light industry, and the range of activity within their walls is remarkable indeed, covering the whole range of light engineering, plastics, food processing, clothing, and hundreds of other industries— enough of these to provide two-thirds of the number of jobs lost in textiles in 1951–61 (at a rough estimate). Thus the old cotton areas have gained something in exchange, but not always equitably as between one area and another, or within the county itself.

By contrast, the major new growth in jobs and population has taken place at the ends of one 'stretch' or axis along the southern limit of the county, commencing at the Manchester Ship Canal with the Trafford Park industrial estate (established in 1897, which now has some 200 factories, warehouses and other industrial premises) and reaching into the suburbs of Liverpool along the line of the East Lancashire Road and the industrial estates at Speke, Aintree and Kirkby. These areas and Merseyside generally have seen a veritably new industrial revolution, with the establishment of motor engineering by Ford, Vauxhall and Standard Triumph, and there are, in the Manchester district (and at Freckleton), aero firms like A. V. Roe. Although the Roe brothers were building aircraft in Manchester before 1914, this is very much a growth industry. A mass of other firms, many of them employing fewer than 500 workers, specialise in 'science-based' products like metallic alloys, radio and radar and scientific instruments. Such industries need huge quantities of steel, and so there are foundries at Irlam and Warrington. Manchester, meanwhile, is a centre for dyestuff products, while chlorine, caustic soda and acids are produced at Widnes. In the St Helens-Warrington localities are glass (Pilkingtons need no advertisement), non-ferrous metal processing, soap and detergent industries.

The industries of Barrow and Furness, soon to become part of the new Cumbria and its economy, have often (rather unjustly) to be mentioned as an afterthought because of their separation. But Lancashire, largely through Barrow's example, will always be remembered in connection with shipbuilding, and the great variety of engineering associated with Vickers-Armstrong.

THE PLANTING AND PLANNING OF TOWNS

The original industrial revolution 'planted' many small mill communities on the county map, places which were clean-slate creations. Belmont near Bolton, Rhodes near Middleton or a railway settlement like Earlestown are good examples. Horwich is an example of several stages of industrial growth, from mill community to railway works. Victorian Lancashire permitted such places to 'just grow' without interference.

Twentieth-century urban areas and new towns can be planned and guided by local and central government, even though actual building may be left to private enterprise and 'developers'. One of the great problems of the county has been 'urban sprawl', vast suburban growth without reference to community sense and amenities—what is the use of living in a bijou bungalow miles from libraries, theatres, cinemas, schools and shops? On the other hand, fields are steadily engulfed, and the Town and Country Planning Acts, operated through the county and county borough councils, have stimulated plans for the maintenance of green belts across central Lancashire. Meanwhile, the housing problems of the towns have often been acute, not least in the form of houses without fixed baths: in Rochdale, Bury, Bolton and Oldham districts the record in 1961 was far worse than the national average in this respect. It has been realised that if new houses are to be built to take 'overspill' from towns, then the sites must be planned.

One of Lancashire's pioneering experiments in this direction was the Manchester suburb of Wythenshawe (1929), which has grown into a vast area with full amenities and a great variety of housing. The new town of Skelmersdale (for which legislation was obtained in 1961), laid out in a former colliery settlement, has been designed to take overspill from Liverpool. Even a carefully designed new town will not always develop community spirit of its own accord, and it has been said that 'Skem' only found its soul when the town developed a successful football team!

Many of Lancashire's real social problems lie to the north-east, and the decision to 'plant' a new town in the Leyland-Chorley area (1965) was partly made with reference to the need for a new growth area away from the successful south, and to the effect of the new M6 motorway, which would make communication with the rest of England so much easier. Although the new town is *not* to be designed for overspill populations, but for the attraction of people, industries and builders by a 'natural' process, it has been feared that the old weaving towns, isolated from this great development, will still be neglected.

THE MODERN GOVERNMENT OF THE COUNTY

Although the Lancashire County Council has an important planning function, much of this is being passed to other areas within the county, with the present-day reorganisation of local government under the terms of the Local Government Act of 1972. In recent years, the major responsibilities have been shared between eighteen county boroughs (the great towns ranging from Liverpool to Barrow in size), and the Lancashire County Council itself. The county authority has administered the needs of 2½ million people, and the county boroughs have looked after another 2½ million souls.

The County Council has become a massive organisation, supervising and helping, until the changeover of 1974, no fewer than 108 second-tier or subordinate authorities (non-county boroughs and urban and rural districts), for which the Council has provided educational, health, welfare, child care, fire, town and country planning and main road facilities. Its budget for the financial year 1973–4 was rather over £259,000,000 of which £165,000,000 was spent on education. But a further £159,000,000 came in the form of government grants.

Under the 1974 reorganisation, the population of the administra-

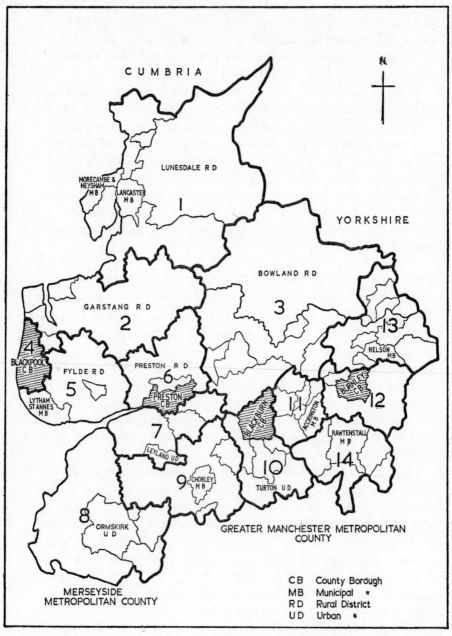

Fig 13A   The new local government areas: the Lancashire administrative county (1974)

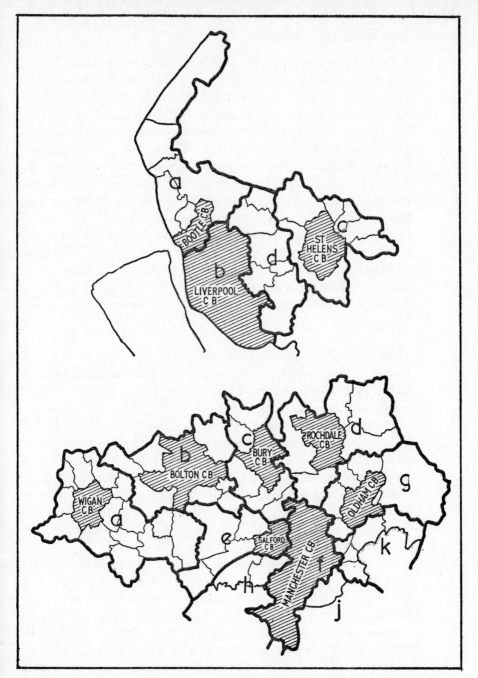

Fig 13B The new local government areas: Greater Manchester Metropolitan County
and that for Merseyside (1974)

tive county of Lancashire is roughly half of the population before that year, and the same applies to rateable values. Two further 'counties', both of them important economic growth areas, have been created: the Greater Manchester Metropolitan County, and the Merseyside Metropolitan County. In addition, Furness is made part of Cumbria, and the Warrington district part of Cheshire. Each new county authority has district councils under it, each of the latter large enough to provide services of high quality. Boundaries are being redrawn in many cases. Whilst the division between very rich and very poor authorities will tend to be narrowed, it is by no means certain that democratic interest in the election of good councillors will be stimulated or served, and local government may appear to be much more remote from many people. This danger is being very partially met by the strengthening of *parish* councils, and by very much enhanced information services.

THE LANCASHIRE SCENE TODAY

Although Lancashire has a firmly established workaday and grimy image, the disappearance of the smoke (under smoke control legislation), and the reconditioning of innumerable terrace houses —picture windows replacing the status symbol of imitation leaded lights—into neatness and brightness, together with the planned renewal of scores of town centres, have altered the county environment in the drabbest of districts. The River Irwell once more gives a home to fish in formerly polluted stretches, and southern visitors to the county are astonished to discover that the Lancashire countryside has beauty and distinction, and that it has corners for relaxation within a few minutes of the great towns.

The claims of Liverpool to be dynamic, as the second British port and as a centre for a people's culture of football, pop or even art, are now well understood, and Manchester will not stay far behind. But much of the debris of the Industrial Revolution remains to be shifted, and the east of the county, with its dank valleys, offers vast problems. The county which helped to pioneer waterways and steam railways has closed many of its branch lines and canals, probably with dire results, and the motor vehicle and its future remains a tiresome enigma. It is not at all clear that the near-destruction of some characterful town centres, and their replacement by steel, glass and chromium, is always in the best interests of people or posterity, and many students of Lancashire ways quite understandably look back into the past for guidance and inspiration. It is hoped that this small book will have helped them to do so.

Social tensions are by no means a thing of the past, and adjustment to Asian settlers in the Lancashire towns has offered its problems. Yet the Irish migrants, for so long objects of animosity, have been absorbed into Lancashire life and have become part of the county's people. In the same way, the newer settlers (despite profound differences of culture) are becoming part of the local scene.

Lancashire, a county which helped to bring about the world's industrialisation, has much leeway to make up in housing, air cleanliness, child and general mortality reduction, the provision of doctors and dentists, and in some aspects of educational and recreational achievement. History does not stand still, and there is much to be done.

SOME GENERAL READING

An excellent study of the evolution of modern Lancashire will be found in Freeman, Rodgers and Kinvig, *Lancashire, Cheshire and the Isle of Man* (1966), and the bibliography in this work cannot be bettered for general purposes. Students in need of detailed economic and population information will find it in the publications of the Lancashire & Merseyside Industrial Development Association, or in the Department of Economic Affairs publication, *The North West* (1965). The *Strategic Plan for the North-West* (1974), issued by the North-West Joint Planning Team on behalf of the government and local planning bodies, is essential for reference.

ACKNOWLEDGEMENTS

Thanks are due to Mr B. J. N. Edwards, Lancashire County Archaeologist, and to Mr Alan King; to Professor H. B. Rodgers; to the late Dr W. Giles Howson; to Mr J. J. Bagley; to Mr I. R. Cowan, Mr J. K. Walton and to Dr W. H. Chaloner; to the Chetham's Library, the Public Record Office, the Lancashire County Record Office, Bolton Public Library, and to the Clerk to Lancashire County Council. None of these individuals or institutions is responsible for any error in this book.

INDEX

Index